The EASIEST KIDS' CRAFTS EVER

The EASIEST KIDS' CRAFTS EVER

Cute & Colorful Quick-Prep Projects
for **Busy Families**

Jacinta Sagona

Creator of Cinta & Co.

PAGE STREET
PUBLISHING CO.

PAGE STREET
PUBLISHING CO.

Copyright © 2021 Jacinta Sagona

First published in 2021 by
Page Street Publishing Co.
27 Congress Street, Suite 105
Salem, MA 01970
www.pagestreetpublishing.com

Distributed by Macmillan, sales in Canada by The Canadian Manda Group.

25 24 23 22 21   1 2 3 4 5

ISBN-13: 978-1-64567-290-6
ISBN-10: 1-64567-290-5

Library of Congress Control Number: 2020948717

Cover and book design by Meg Baskis for Page Street Publishing Co.
Photography by Jacinta Sagona

Printed and bound in China

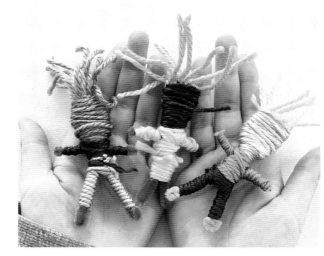

Dedication

To my mum and dad, who taught and encouraged me to craft.

And to Steve, Josh, Isabel and Eliza, who craft and create with me every day.

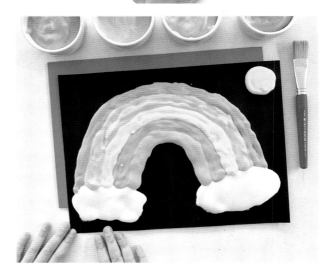

Table of *CONTENTS*

Introduction

Dear Reader,

You might not realize it yet, but you have crafty creativity flowing through your body all the time. And this crafty creativity makes you totally cool and unique. It may seem hidden sometimes, but by putting together the crafts in this book, you will release and explore your creativity and produce some really amazing things! Creativity is so important in all sorts of areas of your life. Crafting will help you gain the confidence to be you and to think outside the box under pressure.

I'm Jacinta, an Australian mother and scientist. Until recently, I worked in a science lab in Melbourne, learning about how our bodies grow and develop. I loved working as a scientist! Now I spend much more time at home with my three young children. And you guessed it—we craft a lot! My mom introduced me to crafting when I was young. I would spend hours happily tinkering away with any materials that I could find.

This book is all about making crafts that are fun, colorful and super easy. You will need only a few easy-to-find materials to create them, and the projects have been designed in such a way that you can do them even if you have little confidence in crafting. Depending on how old you are, you may be able to do many of them all on your own. You can also make these crafts with your friends, and even your whole family!

The projects in this book encourage tinkering, playing and experimenting so you can learn to make amazing things from all kinds of different materials. Mistakes are always allowed! Mistakes push and extend our creativity. We need to make mistakes and try again to get things to work sometimes.

An amazing thing you may have already discovered about crafting is how it can calm you and open your mind. Crafting is relaxing and gives you the opportunity to be mindful. Mindfulness means slowing down to really notice what you are doing. Being mindful is the opposite of rushing and doing lots of things at once. When you are mindful, you take your time and focus in a relaxed, easy way. The activities in this book will allow you to quietly craft away, relax and be mindful.

I really do hope that you LOVE all the crafts in this book! I had so much fun creating them especially for you. I hope that you find them fun and calming, and that they get you experimenting and tinkering away for hours, just like I did when I was younger.

Enjoy,

Jacinta

How to Use This Book

This is a really easy book to use. Simply flip through the pages and choose one of the activities that catches your interest. Start with one that you think is the easiest, then you can gradually work up to some of the more meditative activities in Chapter 6. The activities in that chapter are just as simple and fun, but they might take a little longer to put together and finish.

Each activity includes detailed written instructions, but there are also pictures to help you work through the steps visually. If you're unsure of what to do next, don't be afraid to ask an adult for help! I bet the adults in your life would love to do some of these crafts with you.

While you are crafting, always remember that it's okay if your project doesn't look exactly like the pictures. Just have fun creating your own special versions of these crafts. The final result does not matter as much as the process of creating the craft. Remember to ask yourself lots of questions as you work. Questions like how and why this or that happens can lead to even more experimentation and creativity!

You will notice that each activity includes a scale for messiness, time and adult involvement. This information is super helpful, as it will tell you at a glance how much of a mess you will need to prepare for, about how long the activity will take to complete and how much adult help and supervision will be needed. These details will help you decide which activity will suit the time that you have and space to craft for any given craft session.

Messiness

Approximate Time

Adult Involvement

Master Supply List

This section outlines all the basic items that you will need to do most of the activities in the book. It may seem like a lot of items, but the neat thing is that you probably have most of them at home already. And if you don't, you can gradually build up your supplies as you go. You can easily find these items at your local discount store or craft store. If you need any specific supplies outside of this list to do an activity, I will list them in the activity and tell you where to find them.

Paper and cardboard

Colored construction paper is one of the items used most often in this book. You can buy packs of mixed-color construction paper from department, stationery and discount stores, and even online retailers. Different weights of cardstock are also fun to use. Plain white printer paper is great to have on hand as well.

Warning! A number of the projects in this book call for the use of recycled cardboard boxes. Heavy cardboard can be quite tricky for children to cut and often requires sharp scissors. It is always a good idea to ask an adult for help when cutting cardboard. This will not only protect your fingers from injury but will also ensure that the cardboard is cut accurately and precisely.

Colored pencils, crayons and markers

Colored pencils, crayons and markers are used throughout this book. I always recommend using the washable kind to protect your clothing and workspace. Wearing old clothes while you craft is another way to prevent unwanted stains.

(continued)

Paints and paintbrushes

The activities in this book use paints often. Some projects may call for watercolor paints, while others will suggest acrylic paint. Many brands of washable paint products are available that can be easily removed from clothing. A variety of different-sized paintbrushes will also come in handy. Thick brushes are great for painting large areas, while small, fine brushes are perfect for adding details.

Glue and tape

You will also need a glue stick and white school glue for many of the activities. These glues are safe for children to use, but when using school glue, I recommend having an adult present to help prevent spills. A hot glue gun will also come in handy, but to stay safe, you should leave any hot gluing to an adult. Tape will also be used in many of the activities in this book. I love to use washi tape. Washi tape is a paper tape that is available in bright colors and patterns. It is super easy to use—you can tear it with your hands rather than using scissors. And if you accidentally place it in the wrong spot, you can easily re-stick it elsewhere without damaging your work.

Scissors

I recommend using child-safe scissors—the ones with a rounded tip—when cutting paper and cardstock. Some activities will ask you to cut through thicker cardboard, such as the projects in Chapter 5, or fabric. Cutting thick cardboard or fabric can be difficult and unsafe for children, so ask an adult to do this for you using larger, sharper scissors.

General office supplies

A stapler, hole punch and ruler will be used in some of the activities in this book. You most likely have these at home already. Remember to be especially careful when using your stapler. Be sure to keep your fingers well out of the way of the stapler's jaws to avoid any injuries.

Embellishments

I like to use embellishments such as googly eyes, sequins, pom-poms and buttons often when crafting. I think that googly eyes are my favorite embellishment item ever. They make animals, aliens and monsters look amazing! I also like to use drinking straws in my crafts, particularly paper straws as they are a little more environmentally friendly. They are fun to cut with scissors and look great glued onto paper and cardboard. You will notice that I don't use glitter very often. That's because it is just too messy! We all have one craft item that we don't like as much as others. But if glitter is your favorite thing, by all means use it as often as you like—but please check with an adult first.

Fabric, yarn, felt and ribbon

A small stash of fabric (such as calico), yarn, colorful felt and ribbon is also great to have stored away for crafting. These items can add extra texture and color to your crafts, making them a little bit more special. And it's fun to use scissors on something other than paper. You will learn that cutting paper is very different from snipping fabric, felt and ribbon. Again, remember to use scissors with care. Always check with an adult before using scissors and ask advice on how to cut different materials successfully and safely.

Collecting and Storing Supplies

Neatly organize supplies for craft activities in one area so that you can find them easily. Creating a craft cupboard or even putting together a movable crafting cart will eliminate the mess of hunting for supplies in multiple locations. I like to save glass jars and store small items in them. You can then display these jars on shelves to quickly find what you're looking for. If you are going to store the jars in a box, secure the lids and store them upside down so the jars' contents are visible through the clear bottoms. That way, you won't even have to pick them up to see what's inside!

Recyclables make the best crafting materials. Raid your recycling bin for items such as cardboard boxes, plastic containers, tin cans and glass jars that can be crafted into all sorts of amazing creations. Make sure to clean out plastic containers, jars and cans before using them for crafting. It's a good idea to ask an adult to help you find and prepare recycled items for your crafts. If you have the space in your home, store recyclables for crafting in a box or separate bins so that you always have items on hand for whenever you feel like making something.

Safety and Creative Tips

It is really important that an adult is present to help with crafts that require sharp scissors or a hot glue gun. These items should only be used by an adult. Before you start crafting, read through the activity's materials list and directions with an adult to make sure you have the right materials and can complete the craft safely.

Be prepared for a mess when trying out some of the activities in this book—especially those involving paint. Wearing old clothes is recommended. That way, if you spill any paint or glue on yourself, you don't have to worry about ruining your favorite outfit. It is also a good idea to protect your work surfaces and floors with wipe-clean tablecloths or plastic sheets when crafting—particularly when using paint and markers.

Colorful
PAPER CRAFTS

Paper is one of my family's favorite crafting materials. Not only is paper affordable and easy to find, but it is also super fun to craft with. Paper is available in all sorts of colors, thicknesses, patterns and textures. You can fold, scrunch, snip, paint, curl and twirl, recycle and color it. Paper can also be easily glued so your crafts stick and stay together. With a little creativity, you can do just about anything with paper.

In this chapter, you will learn how to craft a tissue paper sun catcher (page 16) that will look amazing attached to your window and shimmer and shine in the light. You will also learn to create the best-ever solar system mobile (page 32) from only simple crayon shavings and white paper. You can even make a beautiful Mosaic Coral Reef (page 24) from just a couple of paper plates and some colored construction paper!

Paper crafts look amazing displayed in frames on walls and shelves. We often gift our paper crafts to friends and family, adding a personalized touch to birthdays and special occasions. Once you have discovered just how much fun it is to craft with paper, you will surprise yourself with how crafty and creative you can be with it! Let your imagination run wild and get crafting with paper today.

Creative Tip: Don't throw your paper scraps away! Store them in an empty shoebox so you will always have colorful paper on hand to get creative with. These paper scraps and offcuts will be perfect for making the Circle Art Crowns (page 18), Mosaic Coral Reef (page 24) and bendy pyramid activity (page 26) you will find in this chapter.

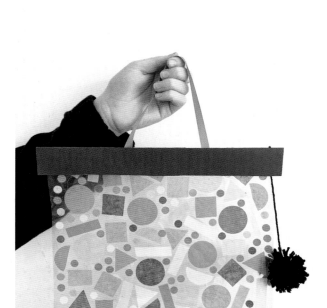

Sticky Tissue Paper Sun Catcher

Everyone will love making and displaying these beautiful sun catchers. Light will shine through the colorful tissue paper shapes, so they are perfect for sticking to windows. You might even like to make a whole series of sun catchers and hang them close together to resemble stained glass.

WHAT YOU WILL NEED

- Colored tissue paper
- Scissors
- 2 (12 x 12–inch [30.5 x 30.5–cm]) pieces clear contact paper
- Hole punch
- String or ribbon
- Tape
- 2 x 12–inch (5 x 30.5–cm) piece black cardstock

LET'S GET CREATIVE!

The tissue paper that's used to make these sun catchers is slightly transparent. That means that light shines through the paper, making colorful shadows. Try making a sun catcher with items that are not transparent, such as sequins, colored construction paper or aluminum foil. By using a mixture of both transparent and non-transparent items, you will be able to play around with light in some really cool ways!

HIDDEN LEARNING!

Reflection and refraction are other import-ant properties of light. When you look in a mirror, you see a reflection of yourself. When you use a magnifying glass to make something small appear larger, it is called refraction. How can you incorporate aspects of reflection and refraction into the next sun catcher that you make?

WHAT YOU WILL NEED TO DO

1. Cut the tissue paper into a variety of shapes. Try cutting squares, triangles or even rectangles. The shapes do not have to be the same size.

2. Remove the backing from one piece of contact paper and place it sticky side up on a flat surface. Press the tissue paper shapes onto the sticky side. Be careful not to make folds in the tissue paper pieces as you stick them on.

3. Remove the backing from the second piece of contact paper and carefully place it, sticky side down, on top of the first sheet of contact paper, sealing the tissue paper pieces inside. Smooth it out with your fingers to remove any air bubbles.

4. Use a hole punch to make two holes in the top of your sun catcher. Thread the string through and tie the ends together to create a hanger.

5. Tape a piece of black cardstock across the top of your sun catcher to cover the holes.

6. To finish, use your scissors to trim a pattern along the bottom edge of your sun catcher. You might like to cut a zigzag or wave pattern. Hang the sun catcher in your window.

Circle Art Crowns

These crowns are perfect for any king or queen to wear! You will have so much fun searching the house for the perfect-sized circles to trace. And then, once you have traced and cut the circles in half, let your creativity go wild coming up with all sorts of cool and amazing designs to decorate your crown with. The little half circles will look like jewels on an actual royal crown!

WHAT YOU WILL NEED

- Circular items
- Pencil
- Colored construction paper
- Scissors
- 1 sheet white paper
- Glue stick
- Ruler (optional)

LET'S GET CREATIVE!

Don't be restricted to circles for your crown! Try cutting squares, triangles or even diamonds. Who knows what sort of amazing patterns you can come up with? And if you're not feeling colorful, try black and white circles. I bet monochromatic crowns would look great too. Also, if you have a hole punch, feel free to use it—they're a great way to make a bunch of tiny colorful circles quickly.

HIDDEN LEARNING!

Are the circle designs you made symmetrical? A shape is symmetrical when both sides look identical. Symmetry occurs regularly in nature and is used in art, design and math—especially the field of geometry. Circles are symmetrical shapes. You can draw a dotted line down the middle, and one side looks identical to the other.

WHAT YOU WILL NEED TO DO

1. Let's go on a circle shape hunt! Search your house for three different-sized circular items to trace. Plastic cups, jars and cardboard tubes are all great items to trace!

2. Once you have found your items, trace around them with a pencil onto colored construction paper. Cut out the circle shapes carefully along the traced lines. You will need to trace and cut out at least six of each size circle.

3. Next, cut the circle shapes in half. It will be fine to eyeball where you should cut, but if you want to get super accurate, you could fold the circles in half first and then cut along the folded line with scissors.

4. Fold a piece of white paper in half lengthwise to mark the midline. Then unfold and smooth the paper out. Cut along the folded line to make two rectangle pieces. Overlap the short edges of the two rectangles, and glue them together. Allow the glue to dry.

5. Using your pencil, and a ruler if you'd like to be exact, draw a line across the white paper that is 2 inches (5 cm) from the bottom edge. Then glue the semicircles down with the cut side facing the line you drew. You may like to alternate circles of different colors and sizes, but always have the cut edge facing the line.

6. Trim the upper edge of the paper into points. Then wrap the crown around your head and cut it to size. Finally, glue the ends of the crown together to secure.

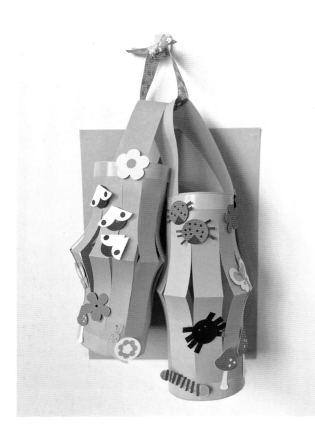

Paper Lantern Garden

Classic paper lanterns are so easy to make and can be decorated for any occasion or event. In this project, you will learn how to make a paper lantern and turn it into an amazing garden scene. You can then string the lanterns together, making a beautiful whimsical garland to decorate a special place in your house.

WHAT YOU WILL NEED

- Ruler
- Pencil
- Colored construction paper (green as well as any other colors you would like)
- Scissors
- Stapler*
- Glue stick

Warning! Ask an adult to help you operate the stapler. You want to protect your fingers from any harm!

LET'S GET CREATIVE!

Once you know how to make a paper lantern, you can transform them into just about any scene that you like. You could make an aquarium with fish and seaweed, or even a zoo scene. You might even like to place the lantern over a battery-operated LED tealight and turn it into a real, functional lantern.

HIDDEN LEARNING!

Also called Chinese paper lanterns, they are made in large numbers to celebrate the Chinese New Year. The first Chinese lanterns were invented in the Eastern Han Dynasty (25–220 AD) and were used to protect the flame within the lantern from windy weather. Chinese lanterns can also be made from silk and sometimes have a bamboo or wood frame to strengthen them.

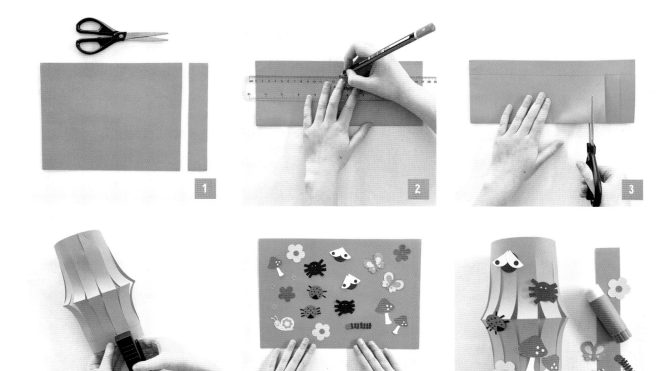

WHAT YOU WILL NEED TO DO

1. Use a ruler and pencil to draw a line that is 1 inch (2.5 cm) from the right-hand side of a green sheet of construction paper. Cut along the line with scissors and put the strip of paper aside. This strip will form the handle of the lantern.

2. Next, fold the remainder of the green paper in half lengthwise. With the fold facing you, draw a horizontal line 1 inch (2.5 cm) from the long edge opposite the fold.

3. Starting at the folded edge, cut a straight line 1 inch (2.5 cm) from the short right-hand edge, all the way to the horizontal line. Continue these cuts along the length of the paper, spacing the cuts approximately 1 inch (2.5 cm) apart.

4. Unfold the paper, then bring the two short edges together and overlap slightly. Ask an adult to secure the top and bottom corners together with staples.

5. Next, take your colored construction paper and draw all of the garden creatures you would like to decorate your lantern with. You might like to draw flowers, butterflies, worms, ladybugs and spiders — anything that you associate with your garden. Using scissors, carefully cut around your drawings.

6. Use a glue stick to paste your garden creatures and decorations onto the lantern.

   Take the paper handle that you made in the first step and glue the ends to the inside of the lantern's top edge. Decorate the handle if you like. You may then repeat these steps to make as many lanterns as you wish.

Washi Tape Cities

Making city skylines from washi tape is lots of fun and a great way to get creative with simple supplies. You can design your own amazing city or replicate a famous city skyline that you know and love. This might be a skyline from your own neighborhood or one from a faraway country. You might even like to include well-known buildings or skyscrapers such as the Burj Khalifa in Dubai, and famous structures such as the pyramids of Egypt. In this activity, we made a nighttime skyline on black cardstock with the moon shining in the background, but feel free to make a daytime skyline if you prefer!

WHAT YOU WILL NEED

- 1 sheet black cardstock
- Washi tape in several colors
- Scissors
- Black marker
- Pencil
- 1 sheet white paper
- Glue stick

LET'S GET CREATIVE!

You might like to add even more detail to your skylines with glitter and stickers. You could add stars and constellations in the sky or even some fireworks with glitter glue to celebrate holidays such as New Year's Eve.

HIDDEN LEARNING!

Currently, the tallest building in the world is the Burj Khalifa in Dubai, United Arab Emirates. It stands 2,717 feet (828 m) high and has been the tallest building since 2010. Historically, the world's tallest man-made building was the Great Pyramid of Giza in Egypt. It held the position of tallest building for over 3,800 years!

WHAT YOU WILL NEED TO DO

1. Place the sheet of cardstock on a flat surface. Unroll a short length of washi tape and press it onto the bottom left-hand corner of the paper, but don't cut it yet.

2. Keep pressing the tape down until it is about two-thirds of the way up the paper. Then use scissors to snip the tape and press the free edge onto the paper to secure.

3. Repeat steps 1 and 2, pressing the next length of washi tape next to the previous tape building. Continue pressing down your buildings, alternating between taller and shorter buildings to achieve the skyline that you like. Alternate the colors of the buildings with different-colored tapes.

4. Use a black marker to decorate the buildings with window and door patterns.

5. Draw a small circle onto the piece of white paper. Cut out the circle and paste it onto the black cardstock, above the tops of the buildings. This will be the moon in your sky. You are all done! Display your beautiful skyline for your whole family to enjoy.

Mosaic Coral Reef

You can create just about any picture or design that you like with a paper mosaic. In this activity, you will turn a simple paper plate into a beautiful mosaic coral reef. You can add all sorts of embellishments that you may have on hand at home to make this as bright and colorful as you like! Just looking at it may transport you to the beautiful coral reefs of Australia and the South Pacific.

WHAT YOU WILL NEED

- Colored construction paper (blue and yellow as well as any other colors you would like)
- Ruler
- Pencil
- Scissors
- Glue stick
- 2 paper plates
- Googly eyes
- Hole punch
- Yarn

LET'S GET CREATIVE!

Paper mosaics also look amazing when they are made from the pages of old magazines and even junk mail, making this a really great recycling activity. You might even like to rip the pieces rather than cutting them to give your piece a really individual look. Think about other craft items you have at home that you could use in the scene. Craft sticks, pom-poms, cotton balls and even cupcake liners would look amazing as part of your mosaic pictures.

HIDDEN LEARNING!

Mosaic art originated in ancient Mesopotamia, where the people used pebbles, shells and stones to decorate temples. Other amazing examples of mosaic art exist in temples and monuments around the world, including St. Mark's Basilica in Venice and St. Peter's Basilica in Vatican City.

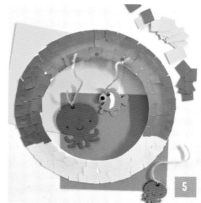

WHAT YOU WILL NEED TO DO

1. On a sheet of blue and a sheet of yellow construction paper, use a ruler and pencil to draw ½-inch (1.25-cm)-wide lines along the length of the papers. Cut along the lines with scissors to form strips. Next, cut each strip of paper into approximately ½-inch (1.25-cm) squares. The squares do not have to be perfectly cut and identical in size.

2. Glue the yellow squares across the bottom of a paper plate to represent sand. Then glue the blue squares above the yellow ones to represent the ocean water. Save some of the squares to use later in the activity.

3. Take pieces of construction paper in other colors and cut them into long strips of seaweed. Glue the seaweed to the floor of the ocean.

4. Next, draw your sea creatures onto colored construction paper. Carefully cut them out and glue googly eyes or draw eyes. Use a hole punch to make a hole in each sea creature. Thread a piece of yarn through and tie to secure, leaving a long tail.

5. Take your second paper plate and cut away the center of the plate, leaving just a frame around the edge. Turn the frame over and glue your remaining blue and yellow paper squares around the edge of the paper plate, yellow on the bottom for sand and the blue on top for water. Use a hole punch to make holes in the top of the paper plate frame. Tie your sea creatures to the frame so they dangle down into the ocean scene.

6. Glue the frame to the edge of your first paper plate. Swish your plate from side to side and watch your sea creatures swim.

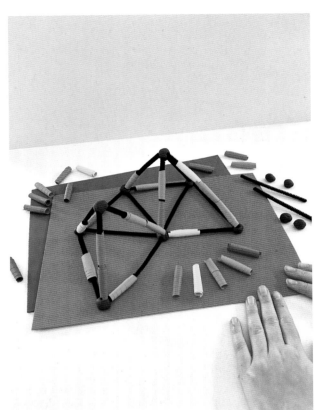

Bendy Pyramids with Paper Beads

Paper beads are super easy and fun to make. They look great hanging from a necklace or bracelet, and even better when used to decorate these amazing bendy pyramids. You will love rolling up the paper beads and threading them onto the pyramids—or towers and any other buildings that you may choose to construct! You may even like to build with a friend. Just imagine the huge scale and size that you could build together!

WHAT YOU WILL NEED

- Colored construction paper
- Pencil
- Ruler
- Scissors
- Glue stick
- Pipe cleaners
- Play dough, modeling clay or putty

HIDDEN LEARNING!

Have you heard of the engineer Gustave Eiffel? Gustave is famous for designing the Eiffel Tower in Paris and for helping to engineer the Statue of Liberty in New York. Do some of your pyramid structures resemble the Eiffel Tower? Perhaps you might like to try and build the Eiffel Tower or another famous building that you are familiar with. And don't just make single pyramids—try joining multiple pyramids together to make giant geometric structures.

LET'S GET CREATIVE!

You can make paper beads from just about any type of paper that you have at home. Try making them from magazine pages, giftwrap or even wallpaper. If you would like your beads to last for ages, have an adult help you waterproof them with clear varnish. Make your beautiful beads as large or as small as you like.

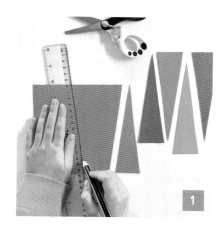

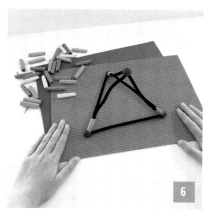

WHAT YOU WILL NEED TO DO

1. Place a sheet of construction paper face down on your work surface. With a pencil and ruler, mark long triangles across the width of your paper as shown. The triangles can be as wide or as narrow as you like. Cut out the pieces.

2. To make a bead, spread glue on one side of a triangle, leaving about 1 inch (2.5 cm) unglued at the wider end. Take your pencil and, starting at the wide end of the triangle, slowly roll the paper around the pencil. By leaving the end unglued, you won't get any glue onto your pencil as you roll.

3. Secure the end of the triangle to the bead with glue. Remove the bead from the pencil and allow the glue to dry. Repeat to make as many beads as you'd like.

4. Start constructing your towers. To do this, take three pipe cleaners and arrange them into a triangle shape. Secure the ends with a ball of play dough or something similar.

5. Next, push a second pipe cleaner into the dough at each corner of the triangle. Thread beads onto each pipe cleaner.

6. Pull the pipe cleaners into a point and secure with a ball of play dough to finish.

Papier-Mâché Animal Sculptures

It is so easy to transform some plain old cardboard and paper into colorful animals to adorn your walls. These sculptures look amazing in groups of three or four on a large wall or as a single larger piece on a smaller wall. I used papier-mâché to give these guys more detail and a 3D feel. Papier-mâché is such a fun technique that every child needs to try at least once, and it only requires newspaper, flour and water.

WHAT YOU WILL NEED

- Pencil
- Recycled cardboard (empty cereal boxes or similar thin cardboard is perfect)
- Scissors
- ⅓ cup (80 ml) white school glue (to make the papier-mâché paste), plus more for adhering items together
- Newspaper
- Ruler (optional)
- 1½ cups (355 ml) water
- 1 cup (125 g) flour
- Paint
- Paintbrush
- Colored cardstock
- Marker

Warning! Papier-mâché can get messy. Please wear old clothes or a smock to craft in, and consider protecting your workspace with newspaper or a tablecloth. This will help make the cleanup easy too!

LET'S GET CREATIVE!

Don't feel limited to making safari animals! You could make giant insects or even weather symbols for the sun, clouds, raindrops and a rainbow. You might like to make a portrait of your favorite person in the world—your mom, dad, sibling, friend or grandparent. Can you imagine their face when you present them with a 3D sculpture of themselves?

WHAT YOU WILL NEED TO DO

1. With a pencil, draw your animal head of choice onto the cardboard and cut the shape out with scissors. When you are shaping your animal face, remember to make it lifelike. Make it pointier for a tiger or zebra and round for a lion or a monkey. Draw and cut out some ears and attach these to the animal head with glue.

2. Next, take a sheet of newspaper and tightly crumple it into a ball. Make three balls and attach them with white school glue to the head for the eyes and nose.

   Tear several sheets of newspaper into strips approximately 2 inches (5 cm) wide, using a ruler to measure if you'd like to be exact.

3. To make your papier-mâché paste, combine the water and flour in a large mixing bowl and stir vigorously. Then add ⅓ cup (80 ml) of white school glue and mix well.

4. Dip the strips of newspaper into the paste and smooth the strips onto your animal head. Continue adding strips of paper until the entire head is covered with a few layers. Let the sculpture dry overnight.

5. Paint the sculpture however you'd like. Allow the paint to dry.

6. Cut whiskers, eyelashes and any hair, fur or mane you'd like from cardstock. Draw any other details like a mouth with marker. Paste them with white glue to the sculpture. Hang your beautiful animal head on your wall! The papier-mâché will be quite light, so you can attach it with double-sided wall tape or sticky tack.

Pom-Pom Blowing Unicorn

Is someone you know having a birthday soon? Surprise them with a pom-pom blowing unicorn to celebrate. These surprise unicorns have clever little catapults attached to the back of their heads that force the pom-poms through the air. You will not believe what that catapult is made from—a balloon!

WHAT YOU WILL NEED

- 1 balloon
- Scissors
- Paper cup
- Tape
- 1 sheet white cardstock
- Black marker
- Colored construction paper
- Glue stick
- Pom-poms
- Confetti (optional)

LET'S GET CREATIVE!

You do not have to make a unicorn; you can make just about anything that you like! You might like to make a confetti-breathing dragon or a marshmallow-roaring lion. All you will need to do is draw the face of the animal, monster or alien of your choice onto the cardstock and then attach the balloon catapult to the back!

HIDDEN LEARNING!

In physics, "force" is a push or a pull action on an object. A force can cause an object to accelerate, slow down, remain in place or even change its shape. In this activity, we stretch the balloon and then let the balloon go. Letting the balloon go forces (or pushes) the stationary pom-poms out of the cup and through the mouth of the unicorn.

WHAT YOU WILL NEED TO DO

1. Start by tying a knot on the neck of the empty balloon. Once the knot is tight, use your scissors to cut off the top half of the balloon.

2. Next, cut the bottom third of the cup away with scissors. This can actually be a little difficult for little fingers, so you may want to ask an adult to help you with this step. Stretch the cut end of the balloon over the bottom of the cup and secure the edge in place with tape.

3. Draw a unicorn head as shown onto the white cardstock and decorate it. I drew an oval shape with black marker. Then I drew the flowers, ears and horn on colored construction paper and cut them out. Finally, I glued the colorful pieces onto the white cardstock.

4. Trace the top of the paper cup onto the mouth area of your unicorn and cut the circle out with scissors.

5. Turn the unicorn head over and tape the top of the cup to the back of the mouth.

6. Fill the mouth with pom-poms and confetti (if using). Pull the knotted balloon end to release the surprise confetti!

Warning! Make sure that a safe distance is maintained before launching the contents of the cup. The pom-poms and confetti are soft but could possibly injure someone's eyes and face if fired at close range.

Melted Crayon Solar Systems

I am sure that you have used crayons to color a drawing, but have you ever melted crayons to make colorful art? Crayon colors look amazing when they mix and melt together. And this is the perfect way to use up all the bits of broken and mismatched crayons that you may have scattered throughout your home. In this activity, you'll learn how to easily and safely melt crayons to make an amazing solar system diorama that will look fantastic decorating any space lover's wall.

WHAT YOU WILL NEED

- Crayons
- Crayon or pencil sharpener
- 1 sheet white paper
- Paper towel, tea towel or cloth
- Iron*
- Pencil
- Scissors
- Colored construction paper
- Glue stick
- White school glue
- Button
- Hole punch
- String
- Beads (optional)
- 2½ x 12–inch (6 x 30.5–cm) strip recycled cardboard

*Warning! Only adults should use the iron to melt the crayons. You do not want to risk burning yourself. And remember that melted crayons can make a mess. Protect both the iron and your workspace with a paper towel, tea towel or cloth.

LET'S GET CREATIVE!

Turn your melted crayons into any artwork you like, including butterflies, flowers and birds. You can even cut the pieces of paper into cards and gift tags or frame them as they are in all their melted color glory. And you don't have to use a sharpener to make the crayon shavings. Try a cheese grater or microplane instead. Remember that the finer your crayon shavings are, the shorter your ironing time will be to melt them.

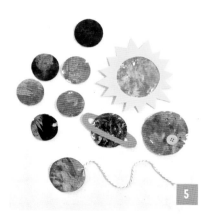

WHAT YOU WILL NEED TO DO

1. Remove any paper labels from your crayons and start sharpening them with the sharpener. Sharpen your crayons into small piles of the same color.

2. Fold a piece of white paper in half and then unfold. Take a few of the shavings and sprinkle them onto one half of the paper. Do not make your layer of shavings too thick; leave some space between the shavings so that they can melt and the colors mix together.

3. Fold the paper over. Place a paper towel, tea towel or cloth over the paper and ask an adult to iron over it to melt the crayon shavings. Use medium-high heat (no steam) and press for a couple of seconds. Allow the melted shavings to cool. If you would like to make different-colored planets, repeat this step with multiple colors of shavings.

4. Next, use a pencil to draw circle shapes onto the paper and cut them out. You will need to draw and cut one sun and nine planets.

5. Cut sun rays from yellow construction paper as well as some rings for Saturn. Attach them to the back of the sun and Saturn using a glue stick. With white school glue, attach a button to form the "eye" on Jupiter.

6. Using a hole punch, make a hole in each planet and the sun. Tie a piece of string to each planet and the sun and thread some beads on if you would like. While you have your hole punch out, punch ten holes across the cardboard strip and attach the loose ends of the planets' and the sun's strings. If you'd like, you can also cut out some stars, an astronaut or even some letters to spell "solar system" or your name to decorate, and tape them to the string of each planet.

Flower Symmetry Drawings

This is a fabulous collaborative activity. You can start by making one half of the flower and then have a parent, sibling or friend finish it. The result is a beautiful piece of art that you did together! It is also a fun way to test your scissor skills. When you look at your finished product, can you tell that it is made up of two different halves, or does it look like one single piece? You might like to sign your side of the artwork as a reminder that it was created by two different people.

WHAT YOU WILL NEED

- Ruler
- Pencil
- 1 sheet white paper
- Scissors
- Construction paper
- Glue stick
- Markers, crayons or colored pencils (optional)

LET'S GET CREATIVE!

You can create other shapes besides flowers. Symmetrical abstract shapes also look great. Simply draw a line down the center of your paper, grab a black marker and make shapes and patterns on the left-hand side of the line. Then have someone else mirror your drawings on the right-hand side of the line. Or you can hide your side and have them draw something totally unique, then compare your two sides to see what is similar and different.

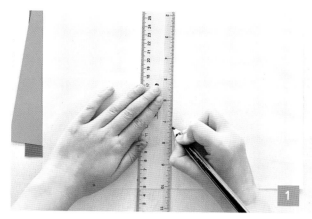

WHAT YOU WILL NEED TO DO

1. With a ruler and pencil, lightly draw a line down the center of the white paper.

2. Draw half a flower on the left-hand side of the paper. Leave the right-hand side of the paper completely blank.

3. Cut petals and flower parts from construction paper to match the size and shape of the flower that you drew. Glue the pieces onto your drawn template. If you do not want to collage your flower, use markers, crayons or colored pencils to draw and color all your flower pieces.

4. Give your half flower to a friend, sibling or parent for them to finish by following steps 2 and 3 on the right-hand side of the picture. You can hide the half that you already decorated by folding it underneath the blank half to encourage them to make something that is their own creative idea. What will they come up with? Open up the paper to reveal your collaborative artwork!

Paint
YOUR OWN FUN

When it comes to making bright and colorful art, you really cannot beat the vibrancy and texture that paint provides. Whether you love painting with acrylic, poster or watercolor paints, you will end up with beautiful art. Paint is one of my most favorite craft materials! You can achieve amazing textures and shades, and when you change up the paintbrushes that you use to paint with, anything can happen. Think about using pom-poms, feathers and even hair combs as paintbrushes to achieve amazing patterns with your paints—let your creativity direct your artwork!

In this chapter, you will learn how to think outside the typical painting box and make your own paints from materials like food coloring and tissue paper. We will explore painting with objects other than paintbrushes to create different patterns and textures. And, we will turn our amazing art pieces into beautiful weavings, letters, mobiles and wall hangings.

One of my favorite activities in this chapter involves taking some plain white printer paper and turning it into a wonderful 3D wall hanging of the moon and stars. You can make this 3D art as bright and colorful as you wish, and even add some glitter for extra twinkle and sparkle. I also introduce you to the magic of tape reveal art and shaving foam puffy paints. Have fun getting creative with paint!

Creative Tip: To avoid a mess, use a dedicated place for painting and set up the area beforehand with protective tablecloths and/or sheets of newspaper. Have everything that you will need for each activity ready before you begin—especially the cleanup materials. Don't forget to have a jar of water to place dirty brushes in and some paper towels or a wet wash cloth handy so that cleanup will be super easy.

Dip Dye Painting

In this project, we'll use everyday food coloring to make vibrant paints. These homemade paints work so well and can be used for just about any art or craft project. They're non-toxic, super affordable (you most likely already have some food coloring at home) and YOU get to decide how much color you would like to add. You can add a small amount of food coloring to make a pastel shade or a larger amount for more vivid colors. The dyed pieces of paper and resulting art piece in this activity remind me of a tie-dyed T-shirt.

WHAT YOU WILL NEED

· Pencil
· Ruler
· 1 sheet watercolor paper or uncoated white cardstock
· Scissors
· Small jars or glasses
· Water
· Food coloring*
· Glue stick
· 1 sheet black cardstock

Warning! Some food coloring brands will stain clothing and work surfaces, so consider wearing an apron or art smock to protect clothing and spreading newspaper or a tablecloth over your workspace.

LET'S GET CREATIVE!

Can you think of any other methods to make your own liquid watercolors? One that I discovered is to take used markers that no longer work well, take the lids off and place each one upside down in a jar with some water. Let the jars sit on a flat surface for a couple of days. You will see that any color left in the markers will bleed into the water, leaving you with an amazing stock of liquid watercolors.

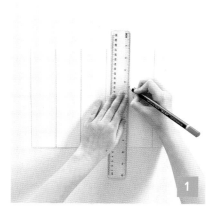

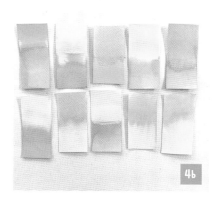

WHAT YOU WILL NEED TO DO

1. With a pencil and ruler, draw lines 2 inches (5 cm) apart across your paper widthwise.

2. Cut along the lines to make strips. Cut each strip into 4-inch (10-cm) lengths.

3. Fill the small jars or glasses halfway with tap water and add one or two drops of food coloring to each jar. Make sure you only add a little food coloring at a time until you reach your desired shade, as a little bit can go a long way. Stir the water to mix in the food coloring.

4. Hold one strip of paper in the water so that the bottom 1 inch (2.5 cm) is submerged and watch as the color rises up the paper. When the color reaches the halfway point, remove the paper from the water, flip it over and dip the undyed end of the paper into a second color. Remove it when the second color meets the first color. Repeat this dye process with all your strips of paper and allow each strip to dry completely.

5. Glue the dried strips of paper onto the black cardstock. You might like to alternate the direction of the strips as you go so that the art piece looks a little like a game of Tetris.

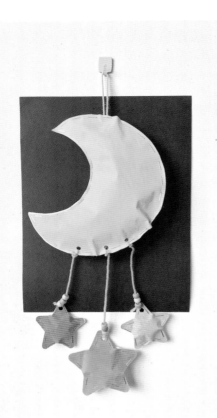

Love You to the Moon and the Stars Wall Hanging

These 3D puffy paper wall hangings will look amazing decorating your walls and would also make a wonderful gift for a loved one. Use as much color as you like when decorating your stars, and you can even add your own little message to your moon and stars to really personalize your design. Where will you display your out-of-this-world wall hanging?

WHAT YOU WILL NEED

- 2 sheets white paper
- Pencil
- Scissors
- Small bowl of water
- Watercolor paints
- Paintbrush
- Stapler*
- Polyester stuffing (or another stuffing material, such as tissues, tissue paper or even newspaper)
- Hole punch
- Yarn
- Beads (optional)

Warning! Ask an adult to help you operate the stapler. You want to protect your fingers from any harm!

LET'S GET CREATIVE!

You could try making a puffy paper weather mobile! How about making a gray rain cloud with blue raindrops hanging from it? A bright yellow sun with colorful paper rays would also look fabulous! Now that you know how to make a puffy paper wall hanging, you can make just about any shape that you like.

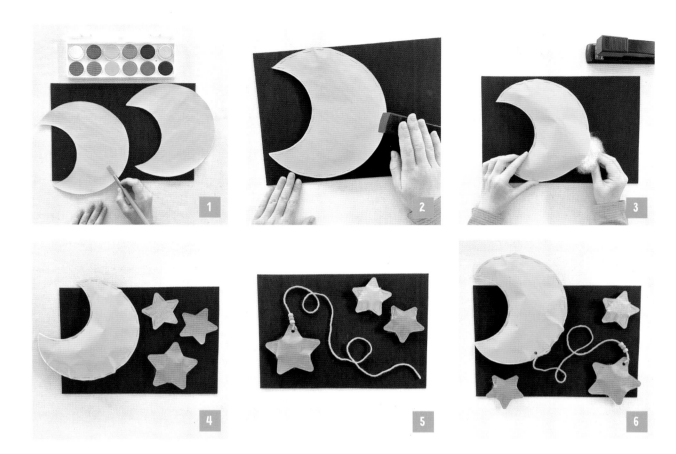

WHAT YOU WILL NEED TO DO

1. Fold one sheet of white paper in half widthwise. Draw a moon shape on one half of the paper. Keeping the paper folded, cut around the moon outline to make two identical moon shapes.

   Paint the moon shapes with your watercolor paints and allow the paint to dry. You can paint both sides of the paper if you like; just let the first side dry before painting the second side. I painted my moon yellow and my stars in bright colors. Feel free to paint yours any color that you like—you might even like to use glittery paint if you have some.

2. Place the moon pieces together. Ask an adult to staple around the edge of the pieces, leaving an open space before they reach the first staple. You will need an opening large enough to add the stuffing in the next step.

3. Carefully fill the moon with a small amount of polyester stuffing, then have an adult staple the remainder of the moon together.

4. Repeat steps 1 through 3 to make your stars.

5. It is now time to assemble your puffy wall hanging. To do this, punch a hole in each of the stars. Thread some yarn through each hole and tie it, leaving a long tail. You might like to thread some beads onto the tail end to give your wall hanging some extra sparkle. But this is totally up to you!

6. Next, make three holes along the bottom of the moon and tie one star to each hole. Have an adult staple a loop of yarn to the top of the moon so that you can hang your beautiful creation.

Paper Weaving

This beautiful weaving activity will turn an ordinary painted piece of paper into an amazing piece of art. You can definitely make one of these pieces on your own, but this is also a really great collaborative project. You might like to make one with a sibling, or when you have a friend over for a playdate. Imagine just how large a piece you could make when working together!

WHAT YOU WILL NEED

- Paints of your choice
- 3 sheets white paper
- Sponge or paintbrush
- Ruler
- Pencil
- Scissors
- Glue stick
- 1 sheet black cardstock

LET'S GET CREATIVE!

After you make this craft, think about what other types of weaving you might like to try. Weaving looms can be made from popsicle sticks and recycled cardboard, and you don't have to just weave paper. Try weaving yarn, ribbon, fabric and even flowers or leaves that you might find in your garden. And don't be restricted to using rectangular looms; you may even like to make a circular loom!

HIDDEN LEARNING!

Weaving is one of the most ancient forms of creativity. Early humans are known to have used fibers from plants to make shelters, fences and baskets. Weaving is still used today to make textiles and fabrics. Large machines do all the weaving work for most of the woven products we use today, but some artists still choose to weave by hand.

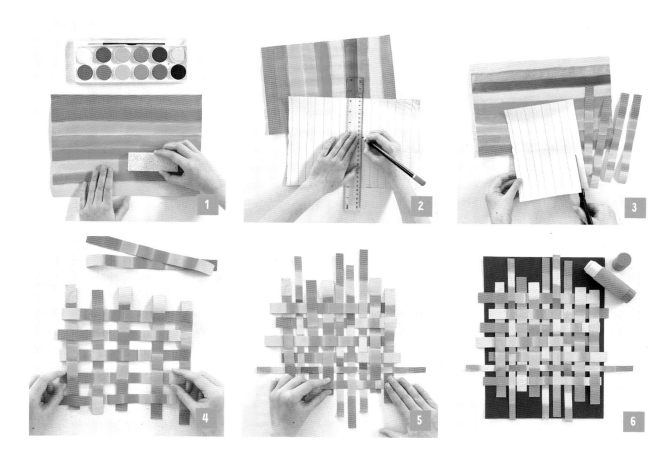

WHAT YOU WILL NEED TO DO

1. Start by painting your three sheets of white paper. You can paint your paper any way that you like, but to get the effect that we did, paint stripes along all three sheets. Paint the stripes lengthwise for two sheets (shown in the photo), and paint the stripes widthwise for the third sheet (shown in the background in photo 2). Allow the paint to dry completely. I decided to apply the paint using a sponge, but you can use a paintbrush or even your fingers.

2. Take your two sheets of paper that have the stripes painted lengthwise. Flip them over so that the painted side is facing down. Use a ruler and pencil to draw 1½-inch (4-cm) lines along the width of the paper, as shown in the photo. Then take your third sheet that has the stripes going widthwise, and on the back draw 1-inch (2.5-cm) lines along the length of the paper. Your pencil lines will be going opposite the direction of the painted stripes.

3. Cut along the lines with scissors. You should now have two sets of strips that are short and thick, and one set of strips that are long and thin.

4. Start weaving the 1½-inch (4-cm) strips together. To begin, take three strips of paper and line them up horizontally. Then take three more strips of paper and weave them vertically over and under the horizontal strips of paper. Continue weaving more strips together until you have used all your pieces.

5. Next, take the thinner strips of paper and weave them through the gaps between the strips you've already woven.

6. Carefully mount your finished woven piece onto the black cardstock with glue.

Stained-Glass Windows

I love the variety of bright colors that tissue paper is available in! It is also super affordable and easy to find—you may even have some that you were gifted as wrapping paper that you can recycle. Using tissue paper makes crafting up a gorgeous project so simple. In this activity, you will use the dye stored in the paper to make paint using only water. It is a magical process and very cool to watch!

WHAT YOU WILL NEED

- Scissors
- Tissue paper
- 1 sheet uncoated white cardstock
- Paintbrush
- Small bowl of water
- 1 sheet black construction paper
- Glue stick

LET'S GET CREATIVE!

Tissue paper is not the only paper that bleeds out color when it's added to water. Try streamers or crepe paper and experiment with which paper sources give you the most vibrant colors. You may even have a paper cutter that you can use to make geometric shapes, such as hexagons, that you can piece together into a pattern. And if you really don't feel like cutting out lots of small pieces, you could tear the tissue paper into pieces, or stack several sheets together and then cut them to speed up the process. This way, you will make lots of different pieces that will blend together brilliantly. Brightly colored precut confetti will work too!

HIDDEN LEARNING!

Have you seen a stained-glass window before? They are often used to decorate churches and other Gothic-style buildings. To make the colored glass, artisans add metallic salts to the glass mixture when heating it. Adding copper to the melted mixture gives the glass a dark red gloss, while cobalt will turn the glass a brilliant blue. Some of the world's most famous stained-glass windows are held in the Sainte-Chapelle chapel in Paris.

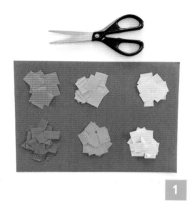
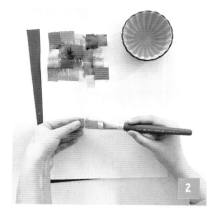

WHAT YOU WILL NEED TO DO

1. Cut the tissue paper into any small shapes that you'd like.

2. Place the white cardstock on a flat surface. Dip a paintbrush into the water and wet a tissue paper piece, making sure that it is fully saturated.

3. Gently press the wet tissue paper onto the white cardstock, making sure the entire piece is attached to the paper. Repeat until you have filled the entire surface of the paper. Allow to dry.

4. Once the tissue paper is dry, gently peel the pieces away from the cardstock. You will be left with colorful shadows of tissue paper dye on the page.

5. Draw and cut out a stained-glass window design from black construction paper.

6. Glue the design onto your dyed cardstock.

DIY Paint Stamps

You will absolutely love making your own stamp designs in this fun activity. You can use ink pads to make your stamp patterns, but I like to use paint. It gives a lovely texture that you can see and feel on your prints. Once you are done stamping a color, simply wipe the stamps clean with a paper towel or cloth and use them over and over again. You can use these stamps to personalize wrapping paper with unique patterns and paint textures.

WHAT YOU WILL NEED

- Scissors
- Recycled cardboard box (an old delivery box is perfect for this activity)
- Ruler (optional)
- Pencil
- EVA foam (or cardboard if you don't have foam)
- White school glue
- Paint
- Paintbrush
- Paper

LET'S GET CREATIVE!

Now that you know how to make a basic stamp, let your creativity run wild and start making all sorts of different stamps. You might like to stick different materials onto your stamp bases such as buttons, beads or pom-poms. And you don't have to limit yourself to just stamping paper. Try applying your stamps to fabrics such as calico, notebook covers or even play dough to make gorgeous patterns.

HIDDEN LEARNING!

A tessellation is a repeating pattern of flat shapes that are fitted closely together without any gaps or overlaps. The Dutch graphic artist M.C. Escher became famous for his tessellations that incorporated recognizable motifs such as birds and fish.

WHAT YOU WILL NEED TO DO

1. Cut the cardboard into 2 x 2-inch (5 x 5-cm) squares. You can use a ruler and pencil to measure the size if you'd like to be exact.

2. Use a pencil to draw a pattern or design onto the EVA foam. I drew a flower pattern consisting of a circular center piece and petals surrounding it. You might like to draw a flower too, or you may prefer to draw leaves, a car or even an abstract pattern like a zigzag or a swirl. Then carefully cut around the outline of your drawing. The foam itself is easy to cut, but if your design is tricky, you might want to ask an adult to do the cutting to make sure that you don't lose any of your detail.

3. Glue the EVA foam pieces onto the cardboard squares and allow the glue to completely dry.

4. Using a paintbrush, carefully apply paint to the surface of your EVA foam cutouts. You can apply it quite liberally, but try to avoid getting any paint on the surrounding cardboard, as any excess paint will end up on your finished print.

5. Once the paint has been applied, gently flip the stamp over and press it onto your paper to make a print. Apply even pressure to the stamp so that the entire stamp pattern is printed, ensuring that you don't shift and smudge your print. Once you are happy with your stamp, gently remove it from the paper by lifting the stamp directly up. You can now reapply more paint and make more stamp patterns, or you can wipe any remaining paint away with a paper towel. Allow any paint remnants to dry, and keep your stamps to use for another day!

Tape Resist-and-Reveal Stars

Tape resist-and-reveal art pieces are quite magical to make. Amazing geometric designs can be created with only washi tape and paint. Apply your tape to the paper, paint and then simply peel the tape away to reveal your masterpiece. You will love making this fun paint-and-reveal shooting star!

WHAT YOU WILL NEED

- Ruler
- Pencil
- 1 sheet white paper
- Scissors
- Washi tape
- Watercolor paints
- Paintbrush

LET'S GET CREATIVE!

Now that you understand the principles of this magical art form, you can make all sorts of amazing art pieces. Try spelling out words or numbers with tape or creating other kinds of shapes, patterns and designs.

HIDDEN LEARNING!

Resist art techniques have been used for centuries. Famous artists have used wax and etching processes to produce beautiful vases, silks and pottery, many of which can be found on display in museums.

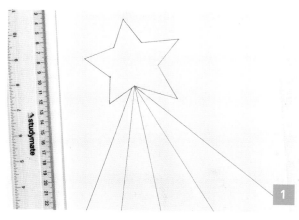

WHAT YOU WILL NEED TO DO

1. Using a ruler and pencil, draw a star shape on the top left-hand side of the paper. Then draw diagonal lines radiating from the star to the edge of the paper.

2. Next, cut off small pieces of washi tape and press them along the lines that you have drawn. You want to cover all the lines, and it is fine if the washi tape overlaps a little.

3. Using watercolor paints, paint the space around the lines of washi tape. Use as many colors as you can, and remember that it is fine if paint ends up on the tape. After all, the tape will eventually be removed. Allow the paint to dry.

4. Very carefully lift the washi tape from the paper to reveal your artwork.

Puffy Paint Rainbows

This amazing puffy paint is made from only three ingredients! You will be sure to have hours of fun with these bright and colorful homemade paints. They're super simple to make, and you can alter the consistency and make as many colors as you like. Puffy paint can be used to create all sorts of artwork like hearts, cute clouds, ice cream cones and even rainbows!

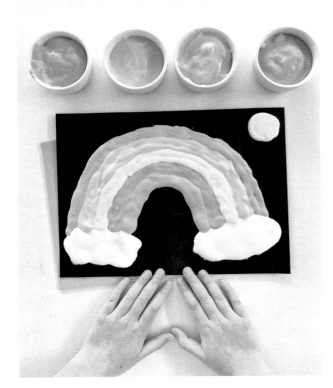

WHAT YOU WILL NEED

- 3 cups (720 ml) shaving cream (not gel)
- 1 cup (240 ml) white school glue
- Mixing bowl
- Spoon
- Muffin tin or mini loaf tin
- Food coloring
- Paintbrush, plastic squeeze bottles or zip-top bags
- 1 sheet cardstock
- Pencil (optional)

LET'S GET CREATIVE!

Take some uncolored puffy paint into the shower or bath to turn bath time into fun time! You could paint with brushes or even your fingers for a real sensory experience. When you are finished, simply drain the tub and rinse the artwork away. And when the weather is nice, try taking your puffy paint outside to paint your pavement!

HIDDEN LEARNING!

Watch the paint as it starts to dry. You may notice that it gets even puffier as it sets and remains puffy to the touch even after it has dried. This is because the air in the shaving cream remains trapped in the glue within the paint mixture.

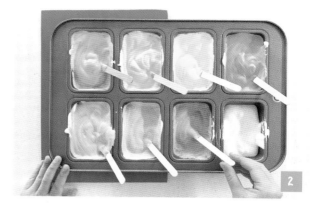
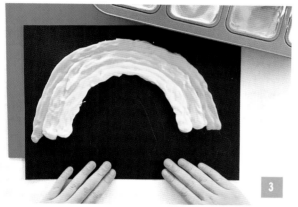
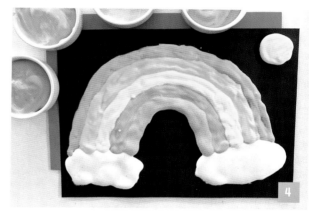

WHAT YOU WILL NEED TO DO

1. Add the shaving cream and glue to a large mixing bowl. Gently mix the ingredients together with a spoon, ensuring that you do not stir the air out of the shaving cream.

2. Divide the puffy paint between the cups in a muffin tin, add a couple drops of food coloring to each and gently stir. Keep adding food coloring until you are happy with your colors. Leave one of the cups of paint white, which you will use for the clouds. Your paints are now ready to use. You can either use a paintbrush to paint directly from the muffin tin onto your paper, or you can transfer the paint to plastic squeeze bottles or zip-top bags using a spoon. If you transfer the paint to a zip-top bag, cut a small hole in one corner of the bag and then squeeze the paint out onto your paper to make puffy lines and dots.

3. Once the paints are prepared to your liking, you can start painting on your cardstock. I painted a rainbow and some clouds with my puffy paint. I started by forming the red outer line of the rainbow and then worked inward, creating the outline of each colored section of the rainbow.

4. Once the outlines were prepared, I went back and filled in the empty spaces with lots of color. I finished the painting with clouds on either end of the rainbow. You may like to sketch out your painting in pencil before you start painting. And if you are feeling really brave, you could even apply the paint with your fingers! This would be messy, though, so you should check with an adult that it's okay first.

Kite Letters

Your friends will love these colorful kite letters when they fly into their mailboxes. The contrast of the black glue and the vibrant watercolors is quite spectacular! The addition of glitter to the glue will give your special letters an extra sparkle and make the person receiving the cards feel extra loved.

WHAT YOU WILL NEED

- 1 sheet white cardstock
- Ruler
- Pencil
- 4 fl oz (118 ml) white school glue
- Plastic bowl (a disposable recycled container will be perfect)
- Measuring spoons
- Black acrylic paint
- Craft stick
- 1 tsp glitter (optional)
- Scrap paper
- Paintbrush
- Watercolor paints
- Scissors
- Yarn or string
- Tape

Note: The blue background and cute cloud shapes are simply for visual effect and are not part of the card. Of course, you are welcome to use a colored piece of paper as your work space, too, to help inspire your creativity!

LET'S GET CREATIVE!

There are so many beautiful art pieces that you can make with just some black glue and watercolor paints or markers. Try making cards, gift tags or even a lovely art piece on a canvas. And you can color the glue with any colored acrylic paint! Try making red, blue and purple colored glues and then create magical underwater scenes, geometric hearts and even landscapes.

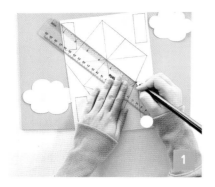

WHAT YOU WILL NEED TO DO

1. Fold a piece of white cardstock in half. Using a ruler and pencil, draw a diamond on the front of the paper. Make sure that the left-hand-side point of the diamond touches the fold. This way, when you cut it out in step 5, the two diamond shapes will stay connected on the left side to make a card. Use the ruler to draw lines along the kite and also some small rectangle shapes for the ribbons.

2. Next, pour the white school glue into a plastic bowl and stir in the black acrylic paint, 1 tablespoon (15 ml) at a time, with the craft stick until you achieve a dark black color and the glue and paint are thoroughly incorporated together. If you'd like to use glitter, add it to the glue and mix again. Ask an adult to help you carefully pour the glue back into the glue bottle and secure the lid.

3. On a piece of scrap paper, practice squeezing out the glue. Draw some lines and try tracing them with the glue to experiment with how it flows from the bottle. Once you are comfortable with the flow of the glue, start tracing along the lines of the kite and ribbons you drew. You will need a steady hand for this, so you might want to ask an adult for help if you're having trouble. Let the glue dry.

4. Once the glue is dry, paint your kite and ribbons with watercolor paint. Allow the paint to dry.

5. Cut around the kite and ribbon shapes. Make sure you leave the left-hand corner joined to the fold so that you can open your kite like a card.

6. Write your letter to a family member or friend. Then tape the ribbon shapes to an 8-inch (20-cm) length of yarn and tape the yarn to the back of the card to finish.

Sunny Bubble Wrap Mobile

Bubble wrap printing is such a fun and easy art technique for kids. And the patterns and colors that you can make using bubble wrap printing are endless! In this activity, we'll make a gorgeous sunny mobile that will brighten your day every time you see it hanging in your bedroom or special place in your house.

WHAT YOU WILL NEED

- Pencil
- 2 sheets cardstock
- Scissors
- Acrylic paint
- Paintbrush
- Small bowl
- Bubble wrap
- Yarn or string
- Tape
- Clothespins
- Black marker

LET'S GET CREATIVE!

Bubble wrap is available in so many different bubble sizes—from tiny bubbles to very large. Feel free to mix up the size of the bubble wrap when you are making your prints and use whatever your family has in the recycling bin. And now that you know just how easy it is to make a beautiful print using bubble wrap and paint, explore the process and make all sorts of shapes and patterns on cards, wrapping paper and gift tags to give your crafts an extra personal touch.

HIDDEN LEARNING!

Bubble wrap printing is a lovely sensory experience that children of all ages can enjoy. A sensory experience is one where you actually get your hands dirty and feel the painting process right through to your fingertips. Feeling the paint with your fingers sends all sorts of messages to your brain about the temperature of the paint and whether you like the feeling or not.

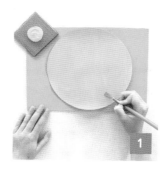   

WHAT YOU WILL NEED TO DO

1. Using a pencil and circular object, trace a circle onto a sheet of cardstock. I traced around a dinner plate that was 10 inches (25.5 cm) in diameter to make my circle. Cut the circle out and paint it with yellow paint. Allow the paint to dry.

2. Add a drop of white paint to some yellow paint in a small bowl and mix it together. Using a paintbrush, spread some of the light yellow paint onto a piece of bubble wrap. I used a piece of bubble wrap that was 5 x 5 inches (12.5 x 12.5 cm). Press the painted bubble wrap onto the yellow circle to leave a print. Continue printing until you have covered the entire surface of the cardstock circle. It is completely fine if some of the prints overlap. Rinse the paint off the bubble wrap so you can use it again in the next steps. Allow the paint to dry. This will be your sun!

3. On another piece of cardstock, paint rectangles approximately 5 x 4 inches (12.5 x 10 cm) in size. Add as much color to the paper as you can. Allow the paint to dry.

4. Using a paintbrush, spread some paint over the surface of the bubble wrap. I chose contrasting colors so that the print would really stand out. Press the bubble wrap onto the painted paper to leave a print. You might like to cover the entire sheet with a print pattern or just a few of the squares. Allow the paint to dry.

5. Once the paint is dry, cut the colorful piece of cardstock into twelve squares. Draw a heart shape onto each square and then cut them out. You will need twelve hearts in total.

6. Next, cut six lengths of yarn and tape them to the back of the sun, leaving the long ends dangling. Tape two hearts to the end of each piece of yarn, one on the front and one on the back.

7. Paint the clothespins yellow and allow the paint to dry. Attach the clothespins around the sun.

8. With a black marker, draw a happy face on the sun. Secure a loop of yarn to the back of the sun with tape. You can then use the loop of yarn to hang the mobile on your wall.

Drip Art

This is a super easy art project that will be loved by older and younger children alike. Making the paint and then watching it drip down the paper is relaxing and fun. Drip art was actually made popular by the famous artist Jackson Pollock. In this activity, we'll use drip art techniques to make a lovely under-the-sea collage.

WHAT YOU WILL NEED

- 1 sheet thick cardstock (or a canvas would be perfect)
- Blue poster paint
- Small bowl
- Water
- Pipette, eye dropper or spoon
- Cupcake liners
- Scissors
- Tissue paper
- Tape
- White school glue
- Googly eyes

HIDDEN LEARNING!

This art technique is a fun way to explore gravity. Gravity is the force that keeps people, cars, houses and other objects on the ground. It also causes objects to fall to the earth, like when you throw a ball into the air or when fruit and leaves fall from trees. In this activity, you're using the earth's gravitational pull to direct the paint from the top of your canvas to the bottom.

LET'S GET CREATIVE!

Don't feel as though the octopus is the only sea creature that you can add to this art piece. Feel free to turn cupcake liners into fish, turtles and other sea creatures. You can make your very own Great Barrier Reef by bending colorful pipe cleaners or scrunching up tissue paper into coral shapes.

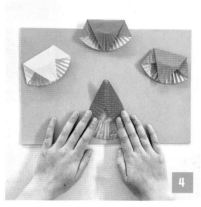

WHAT YOU WILL NEED TO DO

1. Lean your sheet of cardstock up against a book, box or something sturdy. Make sure that you have some newspaper or a tablecloth under the cardstock to collect any drips of paint that run off the paper.

2. Pour some blue paint into a small bowl and add water a little at a time, mixing until it is watered down slightly and will run down the cardstock.

3. Fill a pipette with paint and place the tip at the top of the cardstock. Slowly drop some paint onto the top and then angle it so that the paint will drip down the surface. Keep dripping the paint along the top of the cardstock until you have covered the surface of your paper with the paint. Once

you get the hang of making the paint drips, you can start dripping the paint from the middle of the paper to fill in any gaps that you may have. Allow the paint to dry.

4. Flatten the cupcake liners with your fingers, then fold the sides of each liner in so that they meet in the middle. Fold the pointy end of each liner down to the opposite side.

5. Cut some strips of tissue paper and tape them to the reverse side of the folded cupcake liners. These will be the tentacles on each octopus. Glue some googly eyes onto them.

6. Glue each octopus onto the cardstock. Once the glue is dry, display your beautiful ocean scene!

Handmade
TOYS AND GAMES

Have you ever designed and then made your own toy before? It is such a rewarding process to watch something that you have thought about and designed come to life. Making your own toys is a great way to spend some screen-free time, and the classic toys illustrated in this chapter highlight a number of important scientific principles. But most of all, making these toys is just pure fun! You will be amazed at what you can create. So rather than heading to a store to buy a toy the next time that you are bored, make your own instead!

In this chapter, we will turn just a handful of easy-to-find materials into bright and colorful toys that you can play with over and over again. Your family will love the puppet shows that you act out for them with the homemade theatre and paper silhouette puppets on page 60. And if you don't feel like being in the limelight, you can try getting behind the camera and make an amazing upcycled camera from a recycled box—with its very own drawing board to record what you see through the camera (page 70).

I will also show you how to make your own basketball game (page 72) to test your accuracy shooting hoops and compete against all your friends. You'll even learn how to make a tic-tac-toe game with its own unique carry case (page 78).

You can also test your design skills and make your very own dollhouse that doubles as a fabulous insect or bug hotel (page 62). And who doesn't like playing with cars? In this chapter, I'll show you how to make your very own toy car wash with just an empty milk or juice carton and some paper (page 74). You will have hours of fun both creating and playing with your own toys!

Creative Tip: You can upcycle just about any old household item to make a toy: delivery boxes, cardboard tubes, plastic containers, cups and spoons, even wrapping paper.

Easy Shadow Puppet Theatre

One of my favorite childhood memories was putting on a talent show when family gathered for birthday parties and celebrations. Whether it was a dance concert, magic show or my absolute favorite—a puppet show—I loved putting on a performance. This shadow box puppet theatre is made from a picture frame. The bigger the better! Simply cover the opening of the frame with some tissue paper and then cut puppet silhouettes from black paper. The screen is lit by a flashlight, which projects your puppet shapes onto the paper. Once you have made your theatre, prepare some snacks for your audience and let them enjoy the show.

WHAT YOU WILL NEED

- Picture frame (or make your own by cutting a frame shape from a cardboard box)
- Ruler
- Pencil
- Scissors
- 1 sheet white tissue paper (or parchment paper)
- Tape
- Colored construction paper (green and black as well as other colors you'd like)
- White school glue
- Bamboo skewers
- Flashlight (battery operated or via cell phone)

LET'S GET CREATIVE!

You can make any sort of puppet theatre that you like. You might like to decorate your frame with blue construction paper and make a fun under-the-sea-themed theatre, or turn your puppet theatre into a circus with trapeze artists, a strong man and funny clowns. Or how about a prehistoric dinosaur world, complete with a volcano in the background and all sorts of dinosaurs? You might even like to attach some fabric curtains to give your show a real theatre feeling!

WHAT YOU WILL NEED TO DO

1. Remove the back of the picture frame and any glass, matting and photos. With a ruler, measure the inside of the frame. Cut a piece of tissue paper equal to this size and tape it to the inside of the frame.

2. Cut a strip of green construction paper that is the same length as your frame and 3 inches (7.5 cm) high. If your frame is wider than your paper, tape two or more strips together. Using your scissors, cut 2-inch (5-cm) snips into the paper from the top to make a fringe that mimics grass. Tape the fringe to the bottom of the frame. You may also like to draw and cut out some little garden-themed symbols such as mushrooms, toadstools, birds and flowers using construction paper. Paste them to your frame to further decorate your theatre.

3. Draw your puppet characters onto black construction paper and cut them out. I drew and cut out butterflies, dragonflies, beetles and other animals and insects you would normally find in a garden.

4. Using tape, attach the puppets to the skewers.

5. This puppet theatre actually works best in the dark! To put on your show, sit behind your theatre. You may need to lean your theatre on some books to hold it upright. Then shine your flashlight onto the inside of the theatre to project your puppets onto the screen. You will need to hold your flashlight in one hand and a puppet in the other. Or even better, grab a sibling or a friend and put on your performance together.

Folder Dollhouse

You will not believe how fun and easy it is to put this beautiful dollhouse together. It is made from an everyday paper folder and some colored construction paper. This house is light to carry and super portable. You will be able to take it with you everywhere so that you can play as often as you like! It's perfect for taking on long trips or to cafés and restaurants while you're waiting to eat.

WHAT YOU WILL NEED

- Scissors
- Cardstock file folder
- Markers, paint or crayons
- Colored construction paper
- Ruler (optional)
- Glue stick
- Embellishments like ribbon, buttons and sequins (optional)

LET'S GET CREATIVE!

Don't feel limited to making just a house. You might like to make an apartment building or even an RV or camper that people can travel the world in. If you have some felt on hand, you could make your little dolls and their clothes from it. This will make them more durable and last for more hours of play!

HIDDEN LEARNING!

Did you know that dollhouses were first invented in the seventeenth century and that they weren't built for play? They were actually designed for adults and were closely associated with wealth. The wealthier a person was, the more expensive the miniature objects that were stored within their dollhouse!

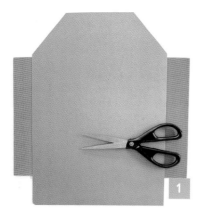

WHAT YOU WILL NEED TO DO

1. Carefully trim the top corners of the folder with scissors so that it resembles a house.

2. Decorate the front of the folder with windows, a door and flowers. You may like to draw the details directly onto the folder with markers, paint or crayons, or even collage the details with colored construction paper.

3. Draw a set of drawers onto a piece of construction paper. My set of drawers is 4 x 6 inches (10 x 15 cm); you can use a ruler if you would like to be exact with your measurements. Cut it out and glue it to the left-hand side of the folder, making sure that you only glue the sides and the bottom to the folder. Leave the top open so that you can store some little paper clothes in the drawers.

4. Next, draw a bed and a pillow on some construction paper, cut them out and glue them to the right-hand side of the folder. Similar to the set of drawers, make sure that you only glue the bottom and the left-hand side of the bed to the folder, so that your little doll can go to sleep. My bed is 4 x 8 inches (10 x 20 cm).

5. Cut a paper doll and some clothes from construction paper. Your paper doll will need to fit into the bed, so make sure that it is not bigger than 4 x 8 inches (10 x 20 cm) if you are following the example. You may need an adult to help you cut out your paper doll.

6. If you'd like, attach a ribbon handle to the top of your dollhouse and decorate with buttons and sequins. Your doll is now ready to play in their house!

Alien Pom-Pom Match Game

These aliens want their eyes back. Their pom-pom eyes, that is! You can whip up one of these fun matching games in just minutes and then test your hand-eye coordination and concentration skills for hours. I used pom-poms to fill the holes, but you can use marbles or any other small bouncy ball that you have at home. You could also really challenge your skills and move multiple pom-poms into place at once.

WHAT YOU WILL NEED

- Scissors
- Empty cereal box
- 1 sheet white paper
- Pencil
- Markers
- Glue stick
- Colored construction paper (optional)
- Pom-poms, marbles or a bouncy ball to play*

*Warning! Always have an adult nearby when you are playing with marbles and bouncy balls to avoid choking!

Warning! Cutting out the alien, especially the holes for the alien's eyes, can be challenging. You may need adult help and supervision with steps 3 and 5.

LET'S GET CREATIVE!

You can make any type of maze game you like, not just one about aliens. Safari animals, portraits of your family members or insects would also be amazing and lots of fun to play with. You might also like to add some numbers to your maze and catch the pom-poms in numerical order for an extra challenge.

WHAT YOU WILL NEED TO DO

1. Very carefully cut away the front of the cereal box, leaving the remainder of the box intact.

2. Draw your alien onto a sheet of white paper with a pencil and color it in with markers. If you are having trouble drawing your alien, you could refer to a picture book with aliens in it to inspire you, or you could ask an adult to find a cute alien drawing for you on the Internet.

3. Cut around the outline of your alien drawing. This might be tricky if you have a lot of detailed edges to cut. You may want to ask an adult for help with this step. You might like to glue your alien onto a piece of construction paper to make your game bright and colorful.

4. Glue your alien drawing to the inside of the box.

5. Cut out the alien's eyes, making sure the eye holes are slightly smaller than the size of the pom-poms that you are going to catch. If the holes are too large, the pom-poms will fall through the holes rather than sit in them.

6. At this point, you might also like to add some extra detail to your alien. You might like to collage or draw spots or stripes onto your alien to make them truly unique. To play, put the pom-poms in the box and move the box around until you catch them in the alien's eye holes.

Monster Stomp

Do you like to dress up? My kids love it! They will dress up as anyone—a fireman, princess, you name it and they dress up as that character. In this activity, you will make your very own pair of monster-themed dress-up "boots," complete with laces to keep them secure on your feet. Practice tying your laces, then wear them to stomp around the house in and have fun!

WHAT YOU WILL NEED

- 1 sheet white paper
- Pencil
- Scissors
- Recycled cardboard
- Paint
- Paintbrush
- Colored construction paper
- Glue stick
- Bamboo skewer
- Shoelaces or ribbon

Warning! Cutting or poking holes into cardboard can be challenging. You may need adult help with step 5.

HIDDEN LEARNING!

Have you heard of the book *Where the Wild Things Are*? It is a great story about a boy and his imaginary monster friend. You might like to read this book before you make this craft, then construct your monster boots to look similar to the monster's feet in the story— bright red with pointy yellow nails!

LET'S GET CREATIVE!

You can decorate your monster boots any way that you like. You could glue on some pieces of yarn or even feathers and make hairy monster feet, or you may choose to draw on some stripes or spots. And dare I say it, but glitter would look great on these too!

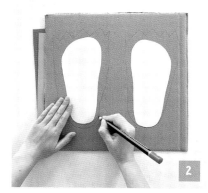

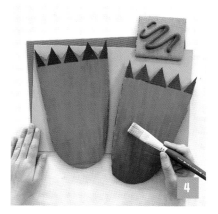
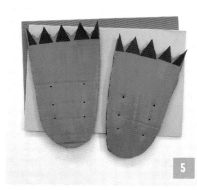

WHAT YOU WILL NEED TO DO

1. Stand on a sheet of white paper and trace around each of your feet with a pencil. Carefully cut around the traced lines with scissors.

2. Place a piece of recycled cardboard on a flat surface and spread your traced foot patterns on top. Using your footprints as a guide, draw the outline of your boots. You will want your boots to be larger than the traced outlines of your feet. Once you have made your drawings, you can remove the tracings. You will not need these anymore.

3. Carefully cut out the boots that you have drawn.

4. Now is the fun part! Decorate your boots with lots of color. You can paint the cardboard and glue down some pointy nails. To make pointy nails, simply draw triangles on a piece of colored construction paper, cut them out and then paste them on the toes of your boots. Once you are happy with your design, allow the paint and glue to dry.

5. Ask an adult to help you make six holes in each boot. I have found that the easiest way to do this is to take a bamboo skewer and carefully push the sharp end through the cardboard.

6. Take your shoelaces or ribbon and lace up the boots. Place your feet in the boots and secure the laces around your feet. Now you are ready to stomp around your house! Stomp carefully at first until you get the hang of walking in your new shoes.

Musical Guitar

This amazing guitar is made of cardboard and has strings made of yarn, so it isn't too noisy and won't disturb your parents—too much anyway! Once you have made your guitar, you might like to make yourself a microphone and start your very own band. What sort of music will you make?

WHAT YOU WILL NEED

- Pencil
- Recycled cardboard (a large delivery box would be perfect)
- Scissors
- Paint
- Paintbrush
- Marker
- White school glue
- 5 buttons
- Ruler (optional)
- Yarn

HIDDEN LEARNING!

Have you ever wondered how guitar strings make sound? Stringed instruments like guitars make notes by vibrating. When a guitar string is plucked, it vibrates, making a sound wave. Depending on how tight the strings are stretched on the guitar, different sounds are made. A string that is stretched tightly will most likely make a very loud sound, while a loosely stretched string will make a softer sound. The weight of the string can also affect the sound that an instrument makes. What sort of sound does your guitar make?

LET'S GET CREATIVE!

Now that you have a guitar, you can make all sorts of other musical instruments to start a band. Try making a microphone and maybe a drum from a recycled tin can or plastic container. And if you would like your guitar to make real plucking noises, try using elastic for the strings instead of the yarn. You can play around with the tension of the elastic (pulling some tight and others loose) to change the sound that each string makes.

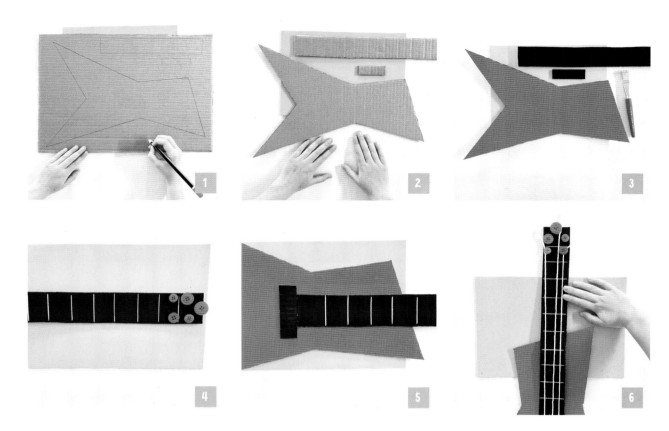

WHAT YOU WILL NEED TO DO

1. With a pencil, draw the shape of a guitar onto a piece of cardboard. You might like to draw an acoustic, electric or even a bass guitar. I decided to draw an electric guitar.

2. Using scissors, carefully cut around the lines that you have drawn.

3. Decorate the body of the guitar. For this step, I used red and black paint, but feel free to add your own colors and make your own guitar as bright and colorful as you like.

4. Next, paint the fretboard of the guitar and add some fret lines with a marker. Glue the buttons onto the fretboard. I glued five buttons to the top: one in the middle of the fretboard and two on either side.

5. Cut a rectangular piece of cardboard that is 2 x 4 inches (5 x 10 cm), using a ruler if you'd like to be precise with your measurements. Paint the rectangle to match the other colors in your guitar (I painted mine black). Make five small snips along the bottom of the cardboard rectangle and glue the piece to the guitar base.

6. Wind the yarn around each button and tie a knot to secure it in place. Pull the yarn down the front of the guitar and secure it to a snip in the cardboard rectangle. Your guitar is now ready to play!

Play Cameras

Are you a budding photographer? If so, a handmade camera might be the perfect toy for you! These cameras are made from recycled boxes and can be decorated any way that you like. Paint yours bright and colorful or make it more realistic looking with some shiny black acrylic paint. My favorite part of this craft is that these cameras have their very own screen on the back where you can draw what you see through the lens.

WHAT YOU WILL NEED

- Small recycled cardboard box (4 x 7 inches [10 x 18 cm] would be perfect, but similar sizes would work too)
- Plastic bottle top
- Paper cup or cardboard tube (such as an empty paper towel roll)
- Acrylic paint
- Paintbrushes
- Hot glue gun* (white school glue will also work, but it may not be as durable)
- Scissors
- Orange cardstock, hole punch and white school glue (optional)
- 1½-foot (46-cm) length of ribbon
- Vinyl chalkboard paper (or white paper if you can't find chalkboard paper)
- Washi tape

Warning! Only an adult should use a hot glue gun. Have them help you with this, or use white school glue instead.

LET'S GET CREATIVE!

Now that you know how to make a simple camera from a recycled box, you might like to add some cellophane to your lens and play around with light. By cutting a hole in the camera face and adding a layer of colored cellophane across the hole, you can look at the world through all different colors!

HIDDEN LEARNING!

Have you ever wondered how a camera works? Light from an object passes into the camera through the lens. If your camera has film in it, the light lands on the film, leaving the picture behind. We don't often use film cameras anymore. Most cameras we use today are digital. In a digital camera, light travels into the camera through the lens, and then lands on a small sensor. This sensor is divided into millions of tiny squares called pixels. The computer in the camera then takes the grid of electrical charges from these pixels and converts them into a picture. Amazing!

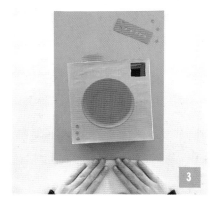

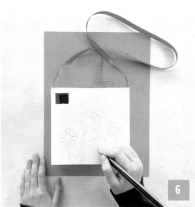

WHAT YOU WILL NEED TO DO

1. Paint the box, the plastic bottle top and the paper cup whatever colors you like, and allow the paint to dry completely.

2. Ask an adult to hot glue the paper cup to the front of the camera box. This will form the lens piece of the camera. Glue the plastic bottle top to the top left side of the camera as the button. If you wish to add some extra detail, use a hole punch to cut a few small circles from orange cardstock and glue them to the bottom left of the camera, or paint them on.

3. Snip a small 1-inch (2.5-cm) square out of the top right-hand corner of the box. Flip the box over and cut the equivalent hole in the back of the box. This will allow you to see through your camera.

4. Ask an adult to hot glue one end of the ribbon to either side of the camera.

5. Cut a piece of vinyl chalkboard paper to size and secure it to the back of the camera with washi tape. Look through your camera and "take a picture." Draw what you see on the chalkboard paper. You can then erase the picture and make a new drawing when you are ready.

6. If you use plain paper as your screen, simply draw on it with erasable pencil so that you can erase your pictures and then redraw your next photograph. Since the paper is attached with washi tape, you might even like to remove your drawing when finished, store it inside your camera box and replace the screen with a fresh piece of paper after each drawing.

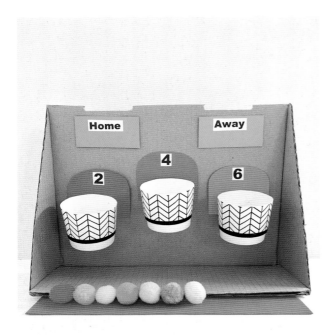

DIY Basketball Court

This DIY basketball court is the perfect game for a rainy-day—or any day! Challenge your friends to a one-on-one tournament and see who can score the most points. You might like to use a timer and see how many baskets you can shoot in a certain amount of time. Who will be the winner of the basketball tournament that you create?

WHAT YOU WILL NEED

- Recycled cardboard box
- Scissors
- Colored construction paper
- Markers
- Washi tape (or regular tape)
- 3 small paper cups or espresso cups
- Ruler (optional)
- Pom-poms

LET'S GET CREATIVE!

These basketball courts would look amazing decorated in your favorite team colors! Which is your favorite team? And now that you know how to make your own sports arena, you can make any sporting arena that you like. You can now take a cardboard box and turn it into a hockey rink or even a football field.

HIDDEN LEARNING!

Try shooting your baskets from different angles. You might like to attach a piece of paper to the bottom of the cardboard box, take a protractor and measure different angles from the goals on the paper. Try shooting from 45- and 90-degree angles. Can you shoot from reflex and acute angles? Which angles are more difficult to shoot from and which ones are easier?

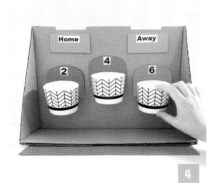
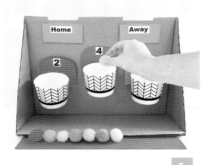

WHAT YOU WILL NEED TO DO

1. Start by cutting the sides off a cardboard box, as pictured. Any size box will work, but I would recommend you find a large rectangular box to give yourself plenty of room to make and play.

2. Next, use markers to make two scoreboards on a sheet of colored construction paper, one labeled "Home" and one labeled "Away." You can either handwrite or type up these labels. Use some washi tape to attach the scoreboards to the back of the box.

3. Draw three backboards and label them with 2, 4 and 6. Using the tape, attach them to the back of the box. These will be the number of points that you score when your pom-pom lands in the basket.

4. Take your scissors and cut the top ½ inch (1.25 cm) off the paper cups, using a ruler if you'd like to be precise. Using some tape, attach the cups to the backboards to represent the nets.

5. Try to shoot a pom-pom into the hoops. Keep track of your score using tallies on the scoreboard.

DIY Car Wash

Children can't get enough of playing with toy cars. Crafting your very own car wash is a great way to make the fun last even longer! In this activity, you will make your very own car wash from an empty milk or juice carton. It's super simple and costs next to nothing, but it will provide hours and hours of play-time fun for you and your siblings or friends.

WHAT YOU WILL NEED

- Large, clean, empty milk or juice carton
- Scissors
- Acrylic paint
- Paintbrush
- Ribbon
- White school glue
- Colored construction paper
- Ruler (optional)
- Paper or plastic drinking straws

Warning! Cutting and snipping the milk carton is quite tricky, so it would be best for an adult to help with steps 1, 3 and 6.

LET'S GET CREATIVE!

Try using different types of fabric, or even foam, that you may have at home to add to your car wash. And for a really amazing time, you could try creating a maze of roads for driving along before you reach your car wash. If you are feeling really crafty, you could even try to make your own cardboard cars to drive through the car wash too!

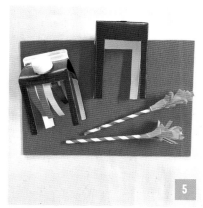

WHAT YOU WILL NEED TO DO

1. Ask an adult to cut the milk carton in half.

2. Paint all four sides and the top of the milk carton with whatever color you would like and allow the paint to dry completely. You may need to apply more than one coat of paint for even coverage.

3. Ask an adult to cut a window in each side of the carton pieces. You can cut any shape windows that you like.

4. Trim lengths of ribbon to match the length of the front window. Attach the ribbons with glue to the opening window of your car wash.

5. Now cut a 2 x 8–inch (5 x 20–cm) strip of colored construction paper, using a ruler to be precise if you'd like. Snip a fringe along the edge of the paper. Wrap this fringe around a drinking straw and secure it with glue. Repeat this step to make a second one. These will form the large sponges that you see in a real car wash.

6. Ask an adult to cut two holes in the top of the milk carton and thread the straws with paper fringes up through the top of the carton.

Now is the time to decorate the outside of your car wash. You might like to make a billboard with some construction paper and attach it to the front roof of your car wash. When your car wash is finished, drive your cars through as often as you like!

Constellation Craft Stick Puzzles

These handmade puzzles can be decorated with any constellation or galaxy that you like and are a fun way to spend a quiet afternoon or morning creating. Once your paint is dry, pop them in a zip-top bag and take them along on holidays and road trips—they won't take much room in your bags—and play with them over and over again!

WHAT YOU WILL NEED

- Craft sticks
- Tape
- Black acrylic paint
- Paintbrush
- Constellation templates (page 146)
- Marker
- Star stickers
- White paint or white gel pen

HIDDEN LEARNING!

A constellation is a group of stars that form a pattern or shape that you can see from Earth. The pattern that they make may resemble the shape of an object, such as a saucepan or crown, an animal or even a mythical creature. There are 88 constellations that light up the night sky! Some of these constellations are only visible from the Northern Hemisphere, such as Ursa Major, while the Southern Cross is a famous constellation, historically used by sailors to navigate by the night sky, that is only visible from the Southern Hemisphere.

LET'S GET CREATIVE!

If you do not have star stickers, you can substitute pom-poms, sequins or even just use a marker or some paint to create your own star shapes. The craft sticks also look amazing with some flecks of splattered white paint to give them a real galaxy feel.

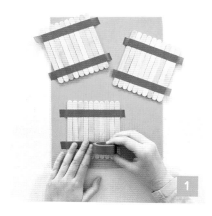

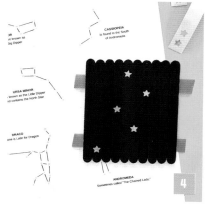
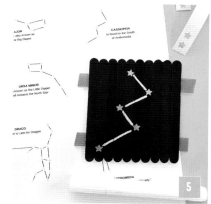

WHAT YOU WILL NEED TO DO

1. Line ten craft sticks up on a flat surface and tape them together. Use two rows of tape, and only apply it to one side of the craft sticks. Each group of ten craft sticks will make one puzzle, and you will paint one constellation on each puzzle.

2. Flip the craft sticks over and paint the entire surface with black acrylic paint. Allow the paint to dry completely.

3. Take a close look at the constellation image in the template. Using a marker, mark dots on the painted surface of the craft sticks to represent each star on the constellation template.

4. Place a star sticker over each of the dots. You will need to make sure that each sticker sits on one single craft stick and not across two.

5. Join the stars with white paint or a white gel pen like a dot-to-dot to finish your puzzle.

6. Remove the tape from the back of the puzzle, mix up your craft sticks and see how quickly you can line them up to put the puzzle back together!

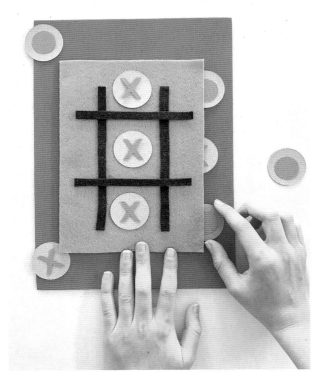

Tic-Tac and Go!

Tic-tac-toe is the best game to play when you are out and about—for instance, while you're in a café waiting for food or while traveling. It's always fun to challenge your family and friends! In this version, you'll make your own felt board that also doubles as a storage container or carry case, and your own personalized playing pieces. Best of all, this game is made from really easily accessible materials and it looks fantastic. You will be able to easily pop this game in a tote bag or backpack for fun on the go.

WHAT YOU WILL NEED

- 2 sheets colored felt, 1 for the board and 1 for the game lines (construction paper if you don't have felt)
- Hot glue gun* (or white school glue if you don't have a hot glue gun)
- 2–4 binder clips or clothespins
- Scissors
- Ruler
- Pencil
- 1 sheet cardstock
- Markers or colored paper and a glue stick, to make the game pieces

*Warning! A hot glue gun works best for securing the felt pieces together. Remember that hot glue guns should only be operated by adults. You do not want to burn your fingers by accident!

LET'S GET CREATIVE!

You do not just have to decorate your playing pieces with X's and O's. You could try decorating them with photos or pictures of different animals, or you might like to use your name to mark the playing pieces. You can also secure the opening of your bag so that the playing pieces do not fall out. Try adding some buttons, or, if you are a super sewer, a zipper would be amazing to prevent any of your beautiful game pieces from getting lost. And now that you know how to make a felt game board, you could try making a larger-scale tic-tac-toe game or even a fun checkers board!

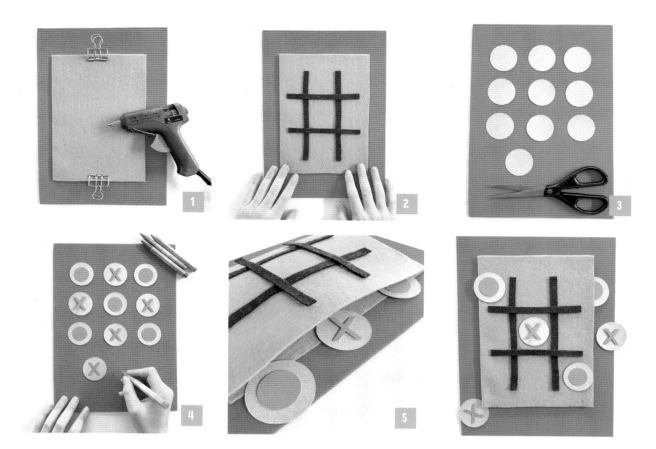

WHAT YOU WILL NEED TO DO

1. Fold one piece of felt in half lengthwise. Ask an adult to secure the top and bottom edges with hot glue, leaving an opening on the side opposite the fold. You may like to lay some paper down under the felt to protect your work surface from glue spills. I have used some red paper to protect my work bench.

   Place the binder clips or clothespins on the glued edges and allow the glue to dry. The clips won't actually stay here—they just help hold the sides together while the glue dries.

2. Cut four ½ x 5-inch (1.25 x 12.5-cm)-long strips of felt, using a ruler and pencil to mark your measurements. Use the hot glue gun to glue the strips of felt in a grid pattern onto one side of your game holder.

3. Draw and cut out ten 1½-inch (3.5-cm)-diameter circles from the cardstock. These will be your game pieces.

4. Label five game pieces with an X and five game pieces with an O. You can use markers to label them, or cut out the symbols from paper and glue them on the circles.

5. Place the game pieces into the storage bag and play whenever you like.

NATURE *Love*

My family loves any excuse that we can find to get out into nature. Whether it be hikes through the mountains, trips to the beach or a scavenger hunt around our local neighborhood, we try to get out as often as we can. While we are out and about, we love to collect all sorts of flowers, leaves, rocks, feathers and amazing things we see and find on our travels. Nature often provides the best craft supplies for gluing, threading and painting. We love to combine our outdoor treasures with traditional craft materials to make lovely creations inspired by nature.

Heading outside into nature also means getting up close and personal with all sorts of bugs and insects. To be honest, I am not the biggest fan of creepy crawly insects, but the ones that we create and study in this chapter are totally my jam! They are bright and colorful, have googly eyes and definitely do not bite. You will have fun creating your very own DIY Bug Catch game (page 82), a cute spider that will actually climb (page 86) and beautiful wish sticks that you can design and dedicate to each of your wishes and dreams (page 92).

You will also create flowers from paper and straws that make the most lovely cards to gift (page 84) and a puzzle toy that looks exactly like a turtle you might find swimming in the waters of the Great Barrier Reef in Australia (page 100). My favorite craft is the cute Family Portrait Planters (page 94). For that project, you will transform an ordinary recycled tin can into a colorful planter that demonstrates the unique characteristics of your family members.

Creative Tip: You don't have to wait for sunny days to get some fresh air. Head outside on rainy or chilly days too. Bundle the family up in warm jackets, hats and mittens and head outside safely. You will find all sorts of inspiring natural craft specimens in all seasons of the year.

DIY Bug Catch

This DIY Bug Catch game is so easy to make and such fun to play. The bugs are made from paper—you can make them as colorful or as realistic looking as you'd like. You'll attach paper clips to them so you can catch the bugs. Use a magnet if you have one at home already, or make your own rod to catch them with. You can even take this bug game outside and enjoy playing in the sun! It is super portable and can be played over and over again.

WHAT YOU WILL NEED

- Pencil
- Markers
- Colored construction paper
- Scissors
- Glue stick
- Paper clips
- Hot glue gun* (optional)
- Tape
- Ruler
- 10-inch (25-cm) length of yarn
- Craft stick
- Pipe cleaners

Warning! To stay safe, if you choose to use the hot glue gun in step 4, it is best to ask an adult to operate it for you.

WHAT YOU WILL NEED TO DO

1. Draw your bug body parts on some construction paper. Generally speaking, an insect or bug body is divided into three major parts: the head, abdomen and thorax. I also drew wings and antennae. You will see that I drew body parts for caterpillars, ladybugs, bees, dragonflies and spiders as well.

LET'S GET CREATIVE!

Now that you know how to make a classic bug catch game, use your imagination to make all sorts of fun catching games! You could make your own fish catching game, or you could even make some colorful animals or butterflies. Try inventing your own tic-tac-toe game where you hook your insects into position on a game board.

HIDDEN LEARNING!

Did you know that insects and bugs are also known as minibeasts? Minibeasts are small animals that do not have an internal skeleton (also called invertebrates). This means that they have their skeleton on the outside of their bodies. There are actually more invertebrates on Earth than any other type of animal. Minibeasts include insects, spiders, worms and snails.

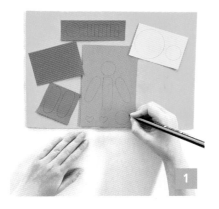

 You can draw all of your favorite bugs, and you can add as much detail as you like. If you would like your bugs to have spots or stripes, draw these details on with markers.

2. Next, carefully cut out all the bug pieces. If some of your pieces are a bit tricky for you to cut out, ask an adult for help so that you don't lose any of the little details that you have drawn.

3. Piece your bugs together with glue. Take your time constructing these little guys so that they resemble bugs that you might see in real life.

4. Then, ask an adult to slightly bend up one end of the paper clip with their fingers. Attach the flat end of the paper clip to your bug with some glue. Using a hot glue gun will secure the paper clips best, but you could also use some tape. Allow the glue to dry. These are the hooks that you are going to use to catch your bugs.

5. To finish your bug catch game, make a rod to catch the little critters with. Tie the yarn to one end of the craft stick.

6. On the other end of the yarn, tie a roughly 2-inch (5-cm) length of pipe cleaner bent into a hook shape. Now it is time to play! Spread your bugs out on a flat surface and use your rod to hook and collect each bug. You might like to time yourself and see how many bugs you can hook in a minute, or try racing a friend or a sibling to see who can catch the most.

Straw Flowers

These straw flowers are bright, colorful and just lovely, as is the little handmade vase that you present the flowers in. You can decorate your vases any way that you like. The flowers would also look amazing on the front of a card, making a beautiful surprise for a special friend! These lovely straw flowers will put a huge birthday smile on your loved ones' faces or will definitely help them feel better soon.

WHAT YOU WILL NEED

- Ruler
- Pencil
- Colored construction paper
- Scissors
- Stapler*
- Hot glue gun* (or white school glue if you don't have a glue gun)
- Paper or plastic drinking straws
- Markers, crayons or colored pencils

Warning! To stay safe, it is best to ask an adult to operate both the stapler and the hot glue gun in this activity.

WHAT YOU WILL NEED TO DO

1. Start by making your flowers. With a ruler and pencil, draw 4-inch (10-cm)-long lines, spaced ¼ inch (6.5 mm) apart onto the colored construction paper. Carefully cut the strips out along the lines. You need twelve strips to make each flower.

   Next, bring the short ends of each paper strip together, without folding the paper, and ask an adult to help you staple the ends together. Each one of these stapled strips is a petal. Repeat with the other eleven strips so you have twelve petals total.

LET'S GET CREATIVE!

Feel free to mix up the colors of your petals. You do not have to make single-color flowers. You could also try mixing different types of paper to give your flowers some texture. Try tissue paper, newspaper and even shiny magazine pages. These would look lovely made entirely from different types of recycled paper and cardstock!

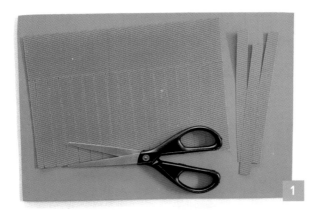

2. Once you have made all the individual petals, gather three petals together and ask an adult to staple them into a small bunch. After each bunch is stapled, bend the excess paper over as shown. You will need four bunches total for each flower.

3. Next, collect four bunches of petals together and ask an adult to staple them. Stapling each bunch of petals together requires a fair amount of strength, so you will definitely need an adult to help you with this step.

   Ask an adult to hot glue the petals onto a drinking straw. Finish your flowers by gluing a circle of construction paper to the center of the petals. This circle will hide all the staples and glue that you used to assemble the flower. I found a small tube that was 1 inch (2.5 cm) in diameter to trace around for circle shapes.

4. Next, make your vase. Simply draw a vase shape on a sheet of construction paper with a marker. You can leave the vase as is or color it with markers, crayons or colored pencils. Cut two slits in the vase that are about 2 inches (5 cm) long. Make sure that these two cuts are at least 2 inches (5 cm) apart. Gently thread your flowers through the slits in the vase to finish. Your flowers should stay in place, but if they don't, an adult can help you secure the straws to the vase with a small amount of hot glue.

Climbing Peg Spiders

How do you feel about spiders? Where I live in Australia, we have many of the world's most venomous spider varieties. Have you heard of a redback spider? They are actually quite deadly—but thankfully we don't really see too many around our house! These climbing peg spiders are much friendlier and cuter than your average redback spider. In fact, I am pretty sure that they will never bite! You will have so much fun making these spiders and helping them climb around your house.

WHAT YOU WILL NEED

- Pencil
- 1 sheet black construction paper
- Scissors
- White school glue
- Googly eyes
- Silver marker
- Ruler
- Paper or plastic drinking straws
- Black washi tape (optional)
- Tape
- Measuring tape
- Yarn
- Wooden clothespins

LET'S GET CREATIVE!

Now that you know how to make a climbing spider, you can make all sorts of magical climbing puppets. Try making dinosaurs, rockets or even portraits of yourself or your family. Play around with size and experiment with making massive or tiny little puppets. You may even like to make two puppets and race them against each other with a sibling or friend. If you have really high ceilings at home, try making puppets on super long strings and see how high yours will climb.

HIDDEN LEARNING!

These simple string puppets are based on an old folk toy. The spider climbs up the strings using friction and alternating tension and slack. You may like to experiment with the angle of the straws to see if it affects how your spider climbs.

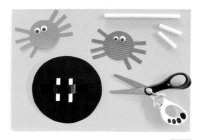

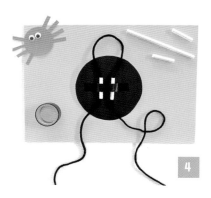
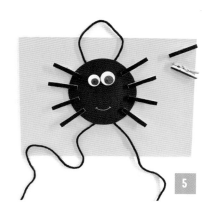

WHAT YOU WILL NEED TO DO

1. Draw circles on a sheet of black construction paper by tracing around a drinking glass or small dish. Carefully cut out the circles.

2. Glue googly eyes onto the circles and use a silver marker to draw a mouth on each.

3. Using a ruler, measure and cut two 1-inch (2.5-cm) lengths of straw and attach them to the back of the circles using tape. I used black washi tape to attach my straw pieces. Any tape will work for this step.

4. Next, measure and cut a 3-foot (1-m) length of yarn. Loop this yarn through the straws.

5. Attach eight clothespins to each circle (the spider's legs) to finish your spider. I covered my clothespins with black washi tape to make a black spider. This is totally optional. You might like to keep your clothespins plain or even color them with markers if you would like.

6. Take the loop in the yarn and hang it over a door handle. Hold one end of the yarn in each hand and pull out and away from the spider. When you let the strings fall, the spider will slide back down to the bottom.

Magical Butterfly House

Have you ever been inside a butterfly house? It is hot and humid, but boy are the ways the butterflies float and fly around in the heat beautiful. In this lovely activity, you will upcycle an old cardboard box into a gorgeous butterfly house with butterflies that you'll decorate yourself and that fly almost magically.

WHAT YOU WILL NEED

- Markers, colored pencils or crayons
- 2 sheets white paper or colored construction paper
- Scissors
- Tape
- An empty shoebox or similar-sized cardboard box
- White cotton thread
- Paper clips
- Small magnets*

Warning! Adult supervision is always required when using magnets.

LET'S GET CREATIVE!

Once you know how to make your drawings fly, you can create all sorts of flying animal or insect scenes. You could decorate your background to look like a beehive and then make little bees to fly around. Or design a forest scene with small colorful birds, or even a fun seaside scene with flying gulls!

HIDDEN LEARNING!

A magnet is a piece of metal that can pull and move other metal objects toward itself. Magnetic forces can work over distance, meaning that a magnet does not always have to be touching an object to pull it—which is exactly what happens in this craft activity.

WHAT YOU WILL NEED TO DO

1. Use markers, pencils or crayons to draw a background scene for your butterfly house onto a piece of white paper. Or you might like to collage a scene with colored construction paper. Next, trim your drawing or collage with scissors to make sure that it fits snuggly inside the shadowbox, then tape it to the bottom of the box.

2. Either draw or collage butterflies on another piece of paper. Then cut around the butterflies with scissors.

3. Cut a roughly 4-inch (10-cm) piece of white cotton thread and tie one end to a paper clip. Secure the other end to the back of a butterfly with tape. Repeat to attach all of your butterflies to paper clips.

4. Place the box on its side so that you are looking into the box and at your background scene. Then place the magnets on the top of and outside the box and move them around to attract the paper clips.

5. Move your butterflies around the box by moving the magnets.

Safari Animal Catch

It is a dream of mine to visit Africa. I would love to see giraffes roam Serengeti National Park and elephants swim in the Zambezi River. Can you imagine being that close to those amazing animals in their natural environment? In this activity, you can get up close with safari animals you have made and then feed them in a fun catching game. Test your own skill and then compete against all your family and friends. Who will have the best aim?

WHAT YOU WILL NEED

- Colored construction paper
- Tape
- Pencil
- Scissors
- Glue stick
- Googly eyes
- Markers
- 7 x 12–inch (18 x 30.5–cm) piece recycled cardboard
- Soft balls, pom-poms or felted balls of wool

WHAT YOU WILL NEED TO DO

1. Roll a sheet of construction paper into a tube and secure it with tape. You will need to roll one piece of paper per animal that you are making.

2. Make the faces for each animal. To do this, draw and then cut the shape of each face from colored construction paper. I drew and cut oval shapes for the giraffe and the zebra, and a circle for the lion. I then collaged brown dots onto the giraffe, white stripes on the zebra and a curly mane onto the lion.

LET'S GET CREATIVE!

You don't need to make just circular tubes with the paper. What do you think would happen if you folded the paper into triangle-shaped tubes or a square-shaped target? Do the different-shaped tubes make it harder or easier to hit the target?

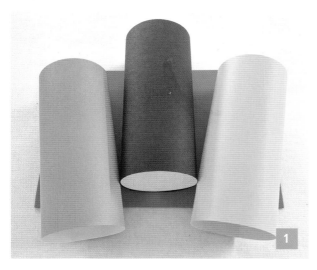

3. Attach each face to its corresponding tube with glue. Glue down some googly eyes. You could also draw any other features that you would like your animals to have like whiskers, stripes or spots with markers.

4. Next, secure the tubes to the piece of recycled cardboard with tape. The cardboard will act as a base plate so that the animals don't fall over as you toss the pom-poms into them.

Place the tubes secured to the cardboard base plate on a flat surface and move about 3 feet (1 m) away. The base plate and the animal tubes together will be the target. Gently toss small balls, pom-poms or anything that you might have on hand into the tubes. Are you able to toss the balls into the target? You can move farther and farther away to make the game more difficult or closer to make it easier.

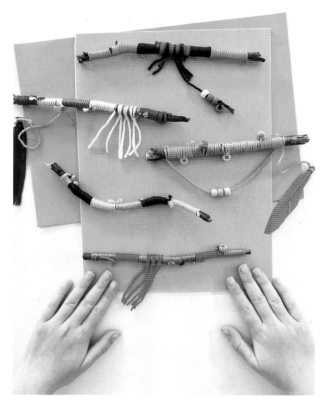

Wish Sticks

It's super easy, and not to mention really fun, to make wish sticks! Simply wrap small sticks that you find outside with yarn, beads and any other craft items that you like, then attach a little handwritten message to your wrapped sticks—something that you wish or dream about happening in your life! Place your wish sticks somewhere special to remind you of all your hopes and dreams that you are working toward.

WHAT YOU WILL NEED

- Sticks*
- Yarn
- Measuring tape
- Scissors
- Embellishments such as beads, feathers or any other decorative craft items you'd like
- White school glue (optional)
- Googly eyes (optional)

*Warning! It is safest to walk with an adult when heading out on a nature hunt. Remember to cross roads safely and always pay attention to cars and bicycle traffic.

LET'S GET CREATIVE!

You can get as creative as you like with the materials that you use to wrap your sticks. You can wrap strips of scrap material or fabric, pipe cleaners and even pieces of ribbon around them. You can also decorate a recycled box from your pantry and turn it into a house to store your wish sticks.

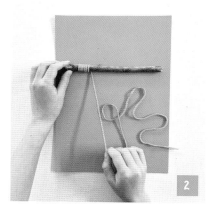
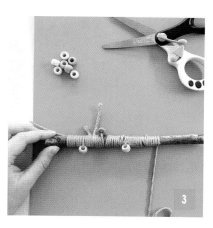
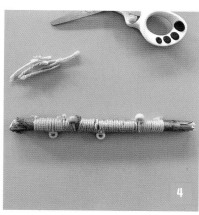
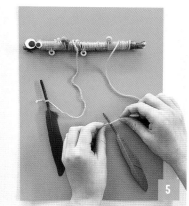

WHAT YOU WILL NEED TO DO

1. Head outside on a nature hunt. Search for a stick that you would like to turn into a wish stick of your own. There is no set size that your wish stick should be. You can make a single, large wish stick or a set of teeny tiny little wish sticks. It is totally up to you. For reference, I have made wish sticks that are approximately 5 inches (12.5 cm) long.

2. The next step is to begin wrapping yarn around your sticks. To start, cut a 12-inch (30.5-cm) length of colored yarn. You can choose any color yarn to wrap your sticks with. Take one end of your yarn and tie it around one end of the stick, securing it with a knot. Then start wrapping the yarn around the stick, making sure that each yarn loop around the stick sits tightly next to the loop before it. You don't want to see too many gaps in the yarn. Once you reach the end of your yarn, tie it off with a knot.

3. Repeat the wrapping process along the length of each stick. You can continue with the same color or cut a new color yarn each time that you finish one length. As you are wrapping the yarn, you might like to thread on some beads for added decoration.

4. When you reach the end of the stick, tie the yarn in a knot and snip off the excess.

5. If you'd like, use some white glue to attach googly eyes and tie some feathers to the sticks with yarn.

Family Portrait Planters

The entire family will love putting together these self-portraits on recycled tin cans. They will look amazing decorating a windowsill, or even sitting on your front doorstep to welcome guests to your home. You can make these planters as realistic as you like by adding glasses, braids and even hair bows. Oh, and fake plants will look just as amazing sitting in the tins if gardening is not your thing!

WHAT YOU WILL NEED

- Acrylic paint
- Paintbrush
- Empty recycled tin cans (labels removed, cleaned and dried)
- Scissors
- EVA foam or colored construction paper
- White school glue
- Washi tape
- Pipe cleaners
- Succulents, plant cuttings or young plants purchased from a garden center
- Potting mix*

Warning! If you are making a planter, remember to use potting mix outside or in a well-ventilated area.

HIDDEN LEARNING!

Most plants require five things to grow: light, air, water, nutrients and space. Plants generally get the light that they need to grow from the sun, although some plants are able to grow under artificial light from a lamp. Plants also need good airflow, regular watering and nutrients found in soil. All living things, including plants, need space to grow. So, please make sure that you select a variety of plant that will be able to survive within the confines of the tin can that you use. Have an adult help you choose just the right plant for your space.

LET'S GET CREATIVE!

Try using all sorts of different materials to make facial features on these planters, such as bottle tops, buttons, straws, googly eyes and beads. These planters would also look amazing with alien heads, robot faces or even your favorite animals.

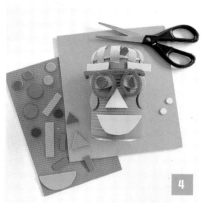

WHAT YOU WILL NEED TO DO

1. Paint the tin cans with acrylic paint and allow them to completely dry. You may need more than one coat to get even coverage.

2. While the paint is drying, cut the EVA foam or construction paper into facial pieces. Cut out a nose, mouth, eyes, eyebrows and any other details you'd like, such as cheeks or eye lashes. Cut one set for each planter you're making.

3. Next, paste the facial pieces onto the tin cans with glue and allow the glue to dry completely.

4. While the glue is drying, cut the washi tape into short strips and press the strips onto the tin cans as hair. Twist pipe cleaners into glasses and attach with glue. This can be tricky! First, fold one of your pipe cleaners in half to mark the center. Then take both ends of the pipe cleaner and twist them to the center. Open the two eye holes to create a glasses shape and then twist one new pipe cleaner to each eye piece to make the ear rests. You might need to trim the length of the ear rests to fit snuggly to the sides of the tin.

5. Finally, head out into your garden with an adult and take a cutting of a succulent or another flower suitable for transplanting. Alternatively, you can visit a garden center with an adult and pick out young plants to put in your planters. Fill the planters with potting mix and gently place your plants into them. Have an adult help you water the plants regularly, and keep them in a sunny location to help them grow.

Nature Weaving

You won't need many items from your craft cupboard to make this beautiful nature weaving, as most of the materials are found outside. Once you have glued your frame together, head outside for some fresh air and collect as many natural specimens as you can find. Then weave them together into one of these spectacular art pieces. These are so much fun to put together that you are going to want to make them time and time again.

WHAT YOU WILL NEED

- Craft sticks
- White school glue
- 1½-foot (45-cm) length of yarn
- Measuring tape
- Scissors
- Flowers (real or artificial), leaves and sticks*

Warning! It is safest to walk with an adult when heading out for a nature hunt in step 5. Remember to cross roads safely and always pay attention to cars and bicycle traffic.

LET'S GET CREATIVE!

You might like to make your loom outside within nature itself. Wrap some yarn between the branches of a tree in your yard and then collect items to weave directly onto the loom! If you do not have a suitable tree to use as a loom, think about constructing your loom out of some sticks or small branches instead of craft sticks.

HIDDEN LEARNING!

The practice of weaving branches, twigs and leaves together dates back almost 12,000 years. Before machines were invented, people wove their own fences, shelters and baskets using natural materials. Weaving by hand rather than machine is now becoming popular again, with many artists making woven rugs, wall hangings and other household items on handmade looms.

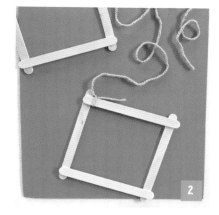
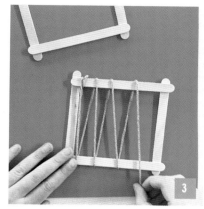

WHAT YOU WILL NEED TO DO

1. Make your loom frame by gluing four craft sticks together in a square shape and allowing the glue to dry.

2. Tie one end of the yarn to the top left-hand corner of the frame.

3. Wrap the yarn around the frame, leaving ½-inch (1.25-cm) spaces between each loop of yarn. This process is called "warping the loom."

4. When you reach the other end of your frame, tie the yarn to secure it and snip away any excess.

5. Next, head outside on a nature hunt. Collect flowers, leaves and sticks that you think would look beautiful in your weaving.

6. Weave and thread your nature specimens through the yarn on your loom. Keep adding items until your weaving is complete! Leave your weaving art on the loom and display it somewhere special in your house, swapping out the flowers and leaves with new specimens as they dry out.

Rainforest Parrot Paperweights

These cute bird sculptures are fun to make and will look amazing on a shelf in your home. You might even like to turn them into lovely paperweights and gift them to a friend or loved one! You can make them as lifelike as you wish. I chose to make these ones bright and colorful—a little like a parrot you might find in the Amazon rainforest.

WHAT YOU WILL NEED

- Pencil
- Recycled cardboard
- Scissors
- Ruler
- Paint
- Paintbrush
- Cotton swabs
- Small piece of orange construction paper
- 1 googly eye
- White school glue
- Craft feathers
- Pipe cleaners
- Tape
- Air-dry modeling clay

LET'S GET CREATIVE!

Don't feel restricted to making just birds. Cats, dogs, butterflies and pet rabbits will also look amazing. Imagine which animal you'd like to have sitting on your desk, holding down a pile of papers while you study on your computer.

HIDDEN LEARNING!

The Amazon is home to over 1,500 different species of birds! The Harpy Eagle is one of the most common birds. These amazing birds can grow to over 3 feet (1 m) tall and have a wingspan over 6½ feet (2 m)!

WHAT YOU WILL NEED TO DO

1. Draw a bird shape on a piece of recycled cardboard and carefully cut it out. Aim to draw a bird that is approximately 6 to 7 inches (15 to 18 cm) high and 3 to 4 inches (7.5 to 10 cm) wide, using a ruler to measure. While these measurements are just a guide, anything larger will prove difficult to stand up in the clay base.

2. Paint your bird however you would like and allow the paint to dry.

3. Dip cotton swabs in paint and dot your bird to decorate it and add detail. While the paint is drying, glue down an orange beak and a googly eye.

4. Glue some feathers onto your bird. I used one large feather.

5. Attach pipe cleaner legs with tape to the back of the bird.

6. To finish your bird, you are going to need to weigh it down. I have found that the best way to do this is with a 2-inch (5-cm) piece of air-dry modeling clay. If you have a large brick of clay, you can ask an adult to cut a piece off the block so you can mold it into a cylinder or cube with your hands. Then, simply press your bird's pipe cleaner legs into the clay to finish your sculpture. Display your sculpture on your desk. When you need to hold a book open or hold down some papers in a pile, use your bird paperweight!

Straw Turtle Puzzle

It is so easy to turn a recycled cardboard box into this cute turtle puzzle. These puzzles are fun to make and will really get you thinking creatively! How many pieces will you fit into your puzzle? Will you paste the turtle shell straws facing in the same direction, or perhaps in opposing directions to really challenge yourself as you're piecing it together?

WHAT YOU WILL NEED

- Pencil
- Recycled cardboard box (12 x 12 inches [30.5 x 30.5 cm] or larger is ideal)
- Black marker
- Green acrylic paint
- Paintbrush
- Scissors
- Ruler
- White school glue
- Paper or plastic drinking straws
- 2 googly eyes

LET'S GET CREATIVE!

These puzzles would also look amazing made into flower shapes or glittery fish that swim in the sea! If you make fish puzzles, you might consider adding some sparkly glitter sequins so that your fish shimmer as though they are actually underwater.

HIDDEN LEARNING!

Do you say turtle or tortoise when you see these puzzles? The major difference between the two is that tortoises live on land for the majority of their lives, while turtles live in water. They have a couple of other differences too, including slightly different shells depending on where they live.

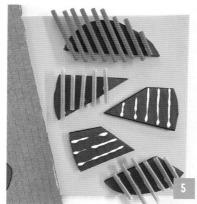

WHAT YOU WILL NEED TO DO

1. Draw the outline of the turtle on the recycled cardboard. I drew the turtle from above, using a pencil so that I could erase any mistakes as I drew. I then traced over the outline with a black marker.

2. Paint the turtle with green paint and allow the pieces to dry completely.

3. Next, ask an adult to cut the shell from the turtle shape. The shell will need to be carefully removed in one single piece. Use a ruler and pencil to draw lines across the shell piece.

4. Carefully cut along the lines on the shell to make your puzzle pieces.

5. Next, glue your straws in lines across the puzzle pieces. Allow the glue to dry completely. When the glue is dry, carefully trim any excess straw length from the pieces with scissors.

6. Glue the googly eyes on the turtle's face. You can now piece the shell back together and play over and over again.

Recycled
CARDBOARD
CREATIONS

I think recycled crafts are some of the best crafts. I love them for so many reasons. To begin with, recycled materials are so easy to come by and cost next to nothing to source. Think about all the empty food boxes and plastic containers, milk and juice cartons, jars and other packaging that you have in your recycling bin. And don't forget about all the bottle tops and lids that go with these containers—they're perfect for crafting with too. I also love the idea of turning something that was headed for the trash bin into something wonderfully colorful and fun.

In this chapter, I'll show you how to turn a piece of recycled cardboard and some yarn into a beautiful weaving self-portrait that you will want to display in your home (page 116), how to create an easy articulated robot (page 118) and how to launch your very own cardboard balloon rocket—just like a rocket launch at NASA (page 110). I'll also show you how to turn an old length of cardboard into a ramp that is perfect for racing cars with your friends and experimenting with all sorts of ways to speed up your cars to make them race faster (page 108)!

Creative Tip: Keep old delivery boxes to turn into the perfect
cardboard creations! As fun as boxes can be for crafting and making all sorts of things, they can be big, bulky and difficult to store. To make storage simple, open the boxes at either end to flatten them, then store them in a cupboard, on a shelf or in a closet. That way, you'll always have cardboard on hand when you feel like creating something, but the boxes won't take up much space at all!

Cardboard Funny Faces

This fun activity is guaranteed to raise giggles and maybe even a few eyebrows! It requires few materials and is a great way to investigate facial expressions and emotions. And at the end, you will have a fun art piece that you made all on your own!

WHAT YOU WILL NEED

- Recycled cardboard
- Pencil
- Scissors
- Colored construction paper
- White school glue
- Stapler* (optional)

Warning! Ask an adult to help you operate the stapler. You want to protect your fingers from any harm!

LET'S GET CREATIVE!

Try turning your funny face into a mask. To do this, make a small hole in each side of the face with a hole punch, attach a piece of elastic or ribbon and then tie it tight to fit around the back of your head. You could make all sorts of funny faces—monsters, zombies or even animals!

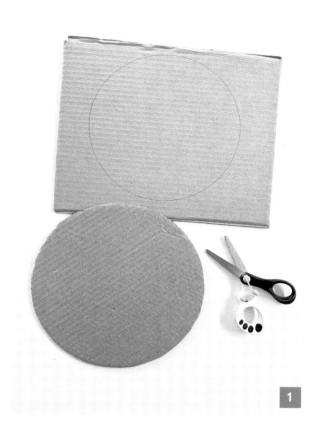

WHAT YOU WILL NEED TO DO

1. Trace around a circular object on a piece of cardboard. You can trace any size circle that you like. I traced a small plate that was 8 inches (20 cm) in diameter to make my funny face. Carefully cut out the circle.

2. Cut the construction paper into strips and then fold, twist and curl the paper into various facial pieces. Get silly with your paper pieces. How about using paper folded like an accordion to make eyes that pop out? Or curly pieces for hair and braids? You could even twist pieces to make wacky ears. You can be as realistic or as abstract as you like!

3. Glue the facial pieces to your cardboard circle. If your pieces are not sticking sufficiently, ask an adult to use a stapler to attach your paper pieces to the cardboard.

Straw Rocket Mazes

Building your very own toy is a fun way to explore engineering and design. No matter how you choose to decorate these maze toys, they're sure to look amazing! They can double as a cool art piece for your walls, as well as being a fun toy that you will play with over and over. Which galaxy or planet will your rocket travel to?

WHAT YOU WILL NEED

- Ruler
- Pencil
- Recycled cardboard
- Scissors
- Tape
- Paint and paintbrushes (optional)
- Paper streamers (optional)
- White school glue
- Paper or plastic straws
- A marble* or small bouncy ball

*Warning! Marbles are a choking hazard. Make sure an adult is with you to supervise when playing with these mazes.

LET'S GET CREATIVE!

What other materials could you use to make the maze? Would play dough, clay or cardboard work the same as the straws? Will using more than one marble at once change the way you move the rocket to complete the maze? You could even turn this into an art activity by dipping the marble in paint and moving it through the maze. A fun mindfulness activity could involve getting a ping-pong ball or pom-pom and blowing the ball through the maze using a straw, taking careful breaths.

HIDDEN LEARNING!

Engineers and designers use science and math to solve different problems. An important step in the design process is testing and changing things that do not work. For your marble maze, think through different locations of the walls to make sure that the marble can run through. The colors that you use and the difficulty level of the maze are also part of the design process.

WHAT YOU WILL NEED TO DO

1. Using a ruler and pencil, draw and cut out a rectangular piece of cardboard that is approximately 8½ x 12 inches (21.5 x 30.5 cm). This will form the body of the rocket.

2. From a separate piece of cardboard, cut three triangle shapes. One 7 x 8½–inch (18 x 21.5–cm) triangle will form the nose cone of the rocket and the remaining two 5 x 12–inch (12.5 x 30.5–cm) triangles will form the fins.

3. Flip the rocket pieces so that they are facedown and secure them together with tape.

4. At this point you might like to paint and decorate the front of your rocket. You can also glue paper streamers on the bottom of the rocket to look like flames. Allow all the paint and glue to dry before moving on.

5. With a pencil, design your maze pattern on the body piece of the rocket.

6. Cut the straws into 1-inch (2.5-cm) lengths.

7. Apply glue to your maze outline, leaving a good amount of glue to ensure the straws will stick. Press the straws into the glue while it's still wet to make your maze.

8. Make sure to glue a border of straws all around the sides to contain your marble in the maze. Allow the glue to dry completely. To play, add your marble at one corner of the maze, tilt to move the marble around the rocket maze and see how fast you can get to the other corner!

Cardboard Racetrack Ramps

This cardboard racetrack can be customized and decorated to your liking and is perfect for racing cars against your friends. It can be used indoors or out and can be easily folded and stored away when you are not using it. The little starting gates are great too and mean that you can race multiple cars at once without anyone getting a head start!

WHAT YOU WILL NEED

- Ruler
- Pencil
- Recycled cardboard
- Acrylic or poster paint
- Paintbrushes
- Tape
- White school glue
- Craft sticks
- Paper or plastic drinking straw
- Pipe cleaner
- Toy cars

HIDDEN LEARNING!

This simple activity is a fun way to explore angles, momentum and friction. Increasing the angle of the ramp will increase the speed at which the cars race down the ramp, but what happens when you race cars with different weights? Heavier cars will usually generate more momentum, which increases their traveling speed down the ramp. Increasing the friction on the track by adding a rough surface will make the cars stick to the track and move more slowly when compared to how they glide across a smooth surface.

LET'S GET CREATIVE!

You can decorate your racetrack any way that you like. Instead of painting colored lanes, you could use black paint to make the road look like asphalt. How can you change the surface of the ramp to change the speed of the cars? Perhaps you could attach some felt or fabric to the ramp to alter the friction. Does this make your cars go faster or slower?

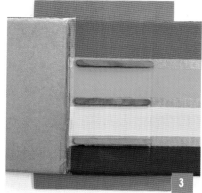
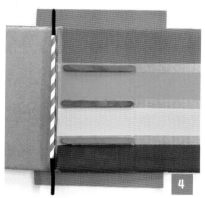

WHAT YOU WILL NEED TO DO

1. Using a ruler and pencil, measure and cut a cardboard square that is 12 x 12 inches (30.5 x 30.5 cm) and a rectangular piece that is 12 x 24 inches (30.5 x 61 cm).

   Paint colored stripes onto one side of the rectangular piece of cardboard to mark the racing lanes on the ramp.

2. Line the pieces of cardboard up next to each other and then tape them together at the edge to secure. You may need a couple of layers of tape to secure them tightly. The square-shaped piece of cardboard will form the stand of the ramp.

3. Glue three craft sticks to the top of the ramp in between each lane to define your starting positions for the cars.

4. Glue the drinking straw to the top edge of the ramp. Thread a pipe cleaner through the straw.

5. Cut a piece of cardboard that is 1 x 12 inches (2.5 x 30.5 cm) and place it on the track. Glue a craft stick to each end of the pipe cleaner, then attach the free ends of the craft sticks to this piece of cardboard. Allow the glue to dry. Glue another craft stick to the left-hand craft stick to make a lever.

6. Line the cars up on the start line. Press the lever to release the cars and start them racing.

Flying Rockets

In this activity, you will design and make your very own rocket and then launch it across a string orbit. These rockets are actually fueled by balloon power!

It is amazing how something as simple as a balloon can move a rocket across the string. You might even like to make multiple rockets and race them against each other. When you have finished launching your rocket, simply detach the rocket from the balloon and the string and display it on a shelf. It will look amazing stored with all your keepsakes, books and special things!

WHAT YOU WILL NEED

- Recycled cardboard tube (such as from a roll of paper towels or toilet paper)
- Aluminum foil
- Tape
- Colored construction paper
- Scissors
- Glue stick
- Tissue paper
- Paper or plastic drinking straw
- String
- Balloon
- Paper clip

HIDDEN LEARNING!

Did your rocket stay upright when it was shooting along the string, or was it too heavy for the balloon to hold up? Did it spin around? How fast did your balloon move along the string? NASA uses rockets to launch satellites into space. These rockets are powered by burning rocket fuel. When the rocket expels the energy produced by burning the fuel, the rocket moves in the opposite direction and lifts off the launch pad.

LET'S GET CREATIVE!

You might like to attach your string to the floor at one end and the ceiling or a door-frame at the other. Is your balloon powerful enough to lift the rocket off the floor? What happens if you use a bigger or smaller balloon? Will a larger balloon allow your rocket to fly for longer than a smaller balloon?

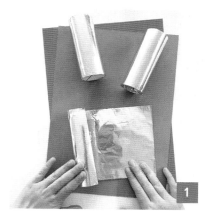

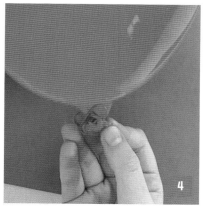
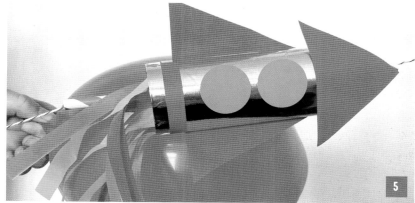

WHAT YOU WILL NEED TO DO

1. Cover the paper tube with aluminum foil and secure the foil in place with tape.

2. Decorate your rocket using pieces of construction paper. Cut out fins, windows and a nose cone and glue them to the tube. Cut strips of tissue paper and secure them with tape to the inside of the tube so they hang out the bottom like flames.

3. Use tape to attach a straw vertically to the back of your rocket. Cut a piece of string approximately 3 feet (1 m) long and thread it through the drinking straw. The exact length of this string is not important, but something around this length will work well. Tie the string to two chairs so that the string is stretched between them.

4. Blow up a balloon and use a paper clip to secure the end so that the air stays in the balloon.

5. Tape the balloon to the drinking straw. Move the rocket to one end of the string and hold the rocket in place. Carefully remove the paper clip and let go of the balloon. Watch the rocket fly along the string!

Kitchen Play Pizza Oven

Small world play is so much fun! In this activity, you will make your own pretend wood-fired pizza oven and pizzas. You might even like to use the oven to create your own restaurant or café setup. Make some menus to go with the restaurant and then "cook" your family's favorite pizzas with all the toppings you can think of. Your mouths will be watering, and you will be craving real pizza for dinner after a long day of playing in your restaurant.

WHAT YOU WILL NEED

- Long, shallow recycled cardboard box for the oven (see step 1 for sizing notes), plus more cardboard for the dials and paddle
- Scissors
- Paintbrush
- Acrylic paint
- White cardstock
- Colored construction paper

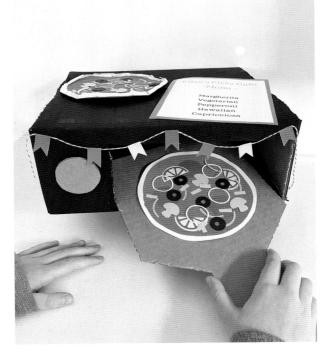

LET'S GET CREATIVE!

Small world play is when children use real-life objects, usually in miniature form, to build stories and play imaginatively. Once you have built your pizza oven, you can set up an entire restaurant using items from around your home. You could play music to set the scene and even dress up in a chef costume.

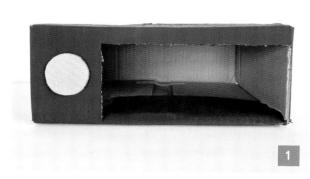

WHAT YOU WILL NEED TO DO

1. To make the pizza oven, you will need a long, shallow cardboard box. I created mine using a 5 x 15–inch (12.5 x 38–cm) recycled box. First, cut out a window from the front of the box with scissors. This is where you will place your pizza to cook. Cutting shapes like this out of cardboard can be tricky, so you may need to ask an adult to help you. Paint and decorate your pizza oven with cardboard dials and knobs.

2. Cut a paddle shape from a piece of cardboard. This is what you will use to place your pizza in the oven and remove it. You can make any size paddle that you like, just make sure that it fits in the window that you cut from the box.

3. To make a pizza, draw and cut out a circle from cardstock, ensuring the circle will fit on the paddle. Paint red paint "sauce" onto the pizza circle.

4. While the red paint is drying, snip colored construction paper into slices of pepperoni, grated cheese, peppers, mushrooms and olives— any pizza topping that you might like. Then sprinkle the toppings onto your pizza and pop it into your oven to cook. There is no need to glue the toppings down. This way, you can re-use the paper food pieces on another pizza creation. You might like to make pizzas to order for your family, friends and even stuffed toys.

Spotty Dalmatian Marionette

These amazing and adorable puppets are made from recycled cardboard tubes that are super easy and inexpensive to come by. Your friends will be amazed when they see these puppets in action. Test your puppeteering skills and see if you can actually make it walk along the floor in front of you.

WHAT YOU WILL NEED

- 1 sheet white paper
- 2 recycled cardboard toilet paper tubes
- Tape
- Scissors
- Bamboo skewer
- Ruler
- 3 (8-inch [20-cm]) lengths white string or yarn
- Beads
- White school glue
- Googly eyes
- Black dot stickers or a black marker
- White pipe cleaner
- 4 craft sticks
- 2 (12-inch [30.5-cm]) lengths white string or yarn

LET'S GET CREATIVE!

Pieces of fabric would look wonderful decorating these puppets, and you could put on a show with them using the Easy Shadow Puppet Theatre on page 60. If you haven't made the puppet theatre yet, simply grab a flashlight and project the shadow of your puppet onto a wall or door in your house. And don't feel restricted to making just Dalmatian dogs; you can make any breed of dog that you like, or any animal for that matter. Simply decorate your tubes to correspond to your chosen animal and finish with details like stripes and whiskers.

 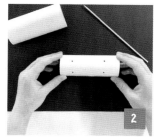 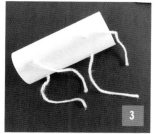 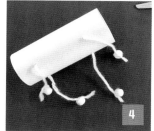

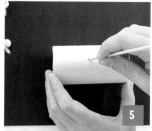   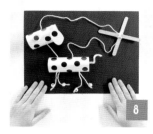

WHAT YOU WILL NEED TO DO

1. Wrap white paper around the cardboard tubes. Secure the paper to each tube with tape and trim any excess paper that may be hanging over the ends of the tube.

2. Ask an adult to help you make four holes in the bottom of one tube using the bamboo skewer, then two holes in the top of the same tube. One hole should be positioned in the center of the tube, and one positioned 1 inch (2.5 cm) from the left-hand side of that hole. (These holes will be used to connect the controlling string and the head piece to the body, respectively.) This first tube will form the body of the dog.

3. Thread an 8-inch (20-cm) piece of string up and through the two holes on the bottom left-hand end of the tube, leaving the free ends of the string to hang down as the legs. Repeat this step with another 8-inch (20-cm) piece of string for the holes on the right-hand side of the tube to form the other two legs.

4. Tie a bead to each free end of the strings and secure with knots. These will be the feet of the puppet. Set this tube aside for the moment while you make the head piece of your puppet.

5. Cut approximately 1 inch (2.5 cm) from the end of the second tube. The longer piece of tube will form the head and the shorter piece can be recycled. Ask an adult to help you make two holes in the tube using the bamboo skewer, one located in the center of the top side of the tube and one located on the underside, 1 inch (2.5 cm) from the right-hand end.

6. Thread an 8-inch (20-cm) piece of string through the hole in the bottom of the head piece and tie to secure. Take the free end of the string and thread it through the hole in the top left-hand side of the body piece tube. Tie with a knot to secure.

7. Glue on some googly eyes and decorate the puppet with spot stickers, or use a black marker to make the dots. Glue a curly pipe cleaner tail onto the dog.

8. Make the handle to control the puppet by gluing two crafts sticks in an X shape and then allowing the glue to dry. Using the two 12-inch (30.5-cm) lengths of string, tie one end of each piece to the handle. Thread the free end of one string through the hole in the top side of the head piece and the other through the remaining hole in the top center of the body piece. Tie knots to secure. Lift up the handle to watch your Dalmatian marionette walk and move around!

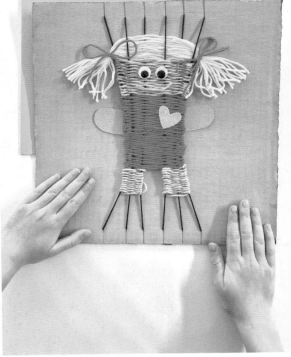

Weaving Portraits

This weaving project will keep you busy and creative for ages. It's the perfect activity for the holidays or a weekend when you have some time to sit down quietly and relax. You can start by painting and decorating the cardboard background any color that you like, and then you can weave yourself or a loved one. Once you get the hang of the over-and-under weaving pattern, you will have no problem making a beautiful art piece. The finished product looks amazing and will deserve a place of pride on a wall or mantel in your home.

WHAT YOU WILL NEED

- Scissors
- Recycled cardboard
- Paint
- Paintbrush
- Ruler
- Pencil (optional)
- Yarn
- Tape
- Craft stick
- Ribbon (optional)
- Googly eyes
- White school glue

WHAT YOU WILL NEED TO DO

1. Cut out a rectangle from a piece of cardboard. The rectangle can be any size, but for reference, mine is 12 x 15 inches (30.5 x 38 cm). Paint the rectangle however you'd like and allow the paint to dry.

2. When the paint is dry, snip across the top and bottom of your loom. Make 1-inch (2.5-cm) snips in the cardboard that are approximately 1 inch (2.5 cm) apart. You can eyeball these snips, or if you want to get super accurate, you can use a ruler and pencil to mark the spots that you need to snip.

LET'S GET CREATIVE!

You can weave just about any shape or pattern on a cardboard loom. Try weaving colorful wall hangings with bright fringes and dangling pom-poms. And if you do not want to weave people, why not try weaving a pet or your favorite animals?

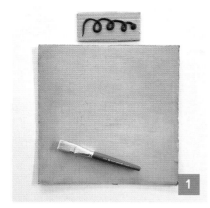
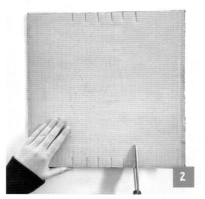
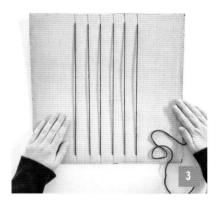

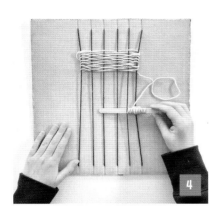
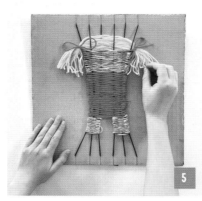
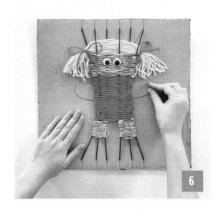

3. Next you will do what is called "warping the loom." First, take some yarn and slip it into the top left-hand corner slit. Use tape to secure the free end of the yarn to the back of the cardboard. Take the other end of the yarn and slip it into the bottom left-hand corner slit. Wrap it around the back of the second snip, then bring it up to the top. Continue wrapping the yarn in this way until you get to the right-hand side of the cardboard. Secure the end of the yarn to the back of the cardboard with tape.

4. To start weaving, measure and cut a 24-inch (61-cm) length of yarn and tie it to the warped yarn where you would like your face to start. Then wrap the free end of the yarn around a craft stick. This craft stick will work like a needle, allowing you to pick the threads that you need to go over and under. Start weaving over and under the warped yarn to form the face shape.

5. Next weave the body, using the same method as in step 4. This just needs to be a rectangle shape. Then weave some legs. Finish by weaving some hair and add some ribbon hair ties if you like. To make pigtails like in this example, weave through 10-inch (25-cm) lengths of yarn and then gather each pigtail into a bow to finish.

6. Glue googly eyes onto the face and cut out some cardboard arms. To make the arms, measure and cut two cardboard rectangles that are 1½ x 5 inches (3.5 x 12.5 cm). Using scissors, curve one end of each piece of cardboard to make a hand. Attach the arms to the back of your woven yarn body with glue. Finish your art piece by cutting a short length of yarn with scissors and gluing it down as a smile. Your woven portrait is now finished and ready to display!

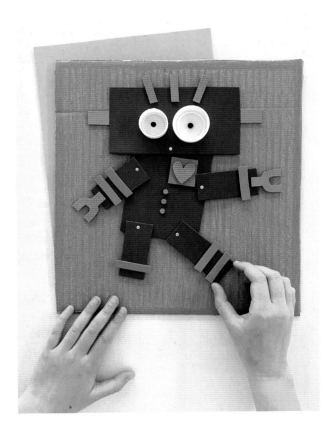

Articulated Robots

You can easily make these cute robots using all sorts of recycled materials collected from around your home. Bottle tops and jar lids will make perfect eyes for your robot, while cardboard boxes and colorful paper scraps will make the best backing and decorations. The really neat thing about these guys is that their arms and legs actually move! These articulated robots will look amazing hung on a wall in your home.

WHAT YOU WILL NEED

- Scissors
- Ruler and pencil (optional)
- Recycled cardboard
- Crayons
- EVA foam (or colored construction paper)
- White school glue
- Hole punch
- 5 metal brads (or 5 [4-inch (10-cm)] lengths of yarn)
- Recycled bottle tops (clean and dry)
- Black marker
- Pipe cleaners to decorate (optional)

WHAT YOU WILL NEED TO DO

1. Cut a rectangular piece of cardboard that is approximately 12 x 15 inches (30.5 x 38 cm). You could use a ruler and pencil to measure, but these measurements do not have to be precise. You can actually make the rectangle as large or small as you like! Decorate the cardboard with your crayons.

   Cut the robot body pieces from the EVA foam as shown in the picture. You will need to cut two large rectangles that will form the head and body of the robot, and four long, narrow rectangles that will form the arms and legs. I have used blue EVA foam to make my robot, but you could use any color.

LET'S GET CREATIVE!

EVA foam is perfect if you want to make a bendy robot like I have. If you do not have EVA foam, you can use construction paper or cardboard instead. Rather than securing your robot to the cardboard backing, you could attach it to a piece of string so that it dangles free. And don't feel limited to just robots. You could make a scarecrow or animals from EVA foam cutouts. Imagine a scarecrow dangling from a string with a fun floppy hat!

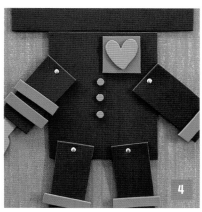
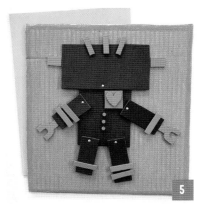
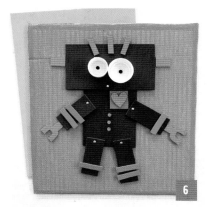

2. You will then need to cut some decorations for your robot. I cut some red and green EVA foam into small rectangles, some hooks for hands and some small circles as buttons. Glue the decorations onto each robot body part as shown in the picture.

3. Next, take a hole punch and make a hole in each arm and leg in the position that it will be attached to the body. Make holes in the body of the robot where the arms and legs will attach.

4. Place a metal brad through the holes in the arms and legs and attach them to the body. If you do not have metal brads on hand, you can use short lengths of yarn and tie the arms and legs to the robot. Tie a knot to secure the pieces and trim away any excess yarn with scissors.

5. Now secure the head piece to the body. To do this, make a hole in the head and the body piece with a hole punch where they will attach. Connect the pieces with a metal brad or tie the pieces together with yarn.

6. Finish your robot by gluing the body piece to the cardboard background. Do not attach the arms and legs to the board, so that they are free to move. Glue the plastic bottle tops to the robot as eyes and draw two black dots to form the pupils. Add pipe cleaner decorations, if using. Allow all the glue to dry completely. Lift up the board and watch your robot come to life!

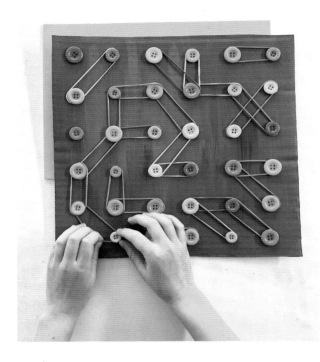

DIY Cardboard Geoboard

You will only need a couple of easy-to-find items to make one of these amazing geoboards. They are a great way to create some awesome art, explore shapes and develop visual skills. They are also perfect for exploring geometry principles like size, area and perimeter. Most importantly though, they are super fun to play with! Once you have constructed your geoboard, you are going to want to play with it over and over again.

WHAT YOU WILL NEED

- Recycled cardboard
- Scissors
- Acrylic paint, markers or crayons
- Paintbrushes (if using paint)
- Ruler
- Marker
- Hot glue gun* (or white school glue if you don't have a glue gun)
- Buttons (see Let's Get Creative! tip)
- Elastic bands

Warning! Only an adult should use a hot glue gun. Have an adult help you, or use white school glue instead.

LET'S GET CREATIVE!

If you do not have buttons, or if you think that you might find it tricky to glue them down successfully, you could use small wooden blocks or beads in place of the buttons. Also, you don't have to use only elastic bands. You can also wrap yarn around the buttons and weave all sorts of shapes and patterns. Once you've created your shapes and patterns, you might like to place some pom-poms in the spaces between the bands or yarn and retrieve them with tweezers, trying not to touch the bands as you go—a little like your own DIY version of the game Operation!

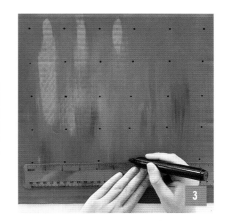
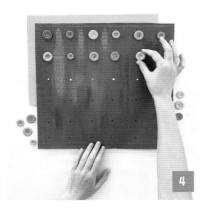
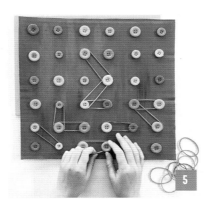

WHAT YOU WILL NEED TO DO

1. Cut the cardboard into a square, or whatever shape you would like. I made a geoboard that is a 17 x 17–inch (45 x 45–cm) square, but you can make yours any size, depending on the size of the cardboard you have available.

2. Decorate the geoboard however you'd like using paints, markers or crayons. I painted my geoboard with bright acrylic paint. If you choose to paint your board, make sure that you let the paint dry before moving on to step 3.

3. Use a ruler and a marker to mark spaces all over the geoboard that are 1 inch (2.5 cm) apart.

4. Ask an adult to place a small drop of hot glue onto each mark, using the hot glue gun (or use school glue) and then press a button onto the drop. Make sure that only the center of the button is glued. Leave the edge of the button free from glue. Repeat until all the marks have buttons on them. Let the glue dry completely.

5. Wrap elastic bands around the buttons to make shapes, letters and all sorts of interesting patterns.

Magical Cardboard Thaumatrope

A thaumatrope is an optical illusion toy where a disk with a picture drawn on each side is attached to two pieces of string. When the strings are quickly twirled between your fingers, the two pictures appear to blend into one. A thaumatrope is SO easy to make. They only take a couple of minutes to put together, and the possibilities of what you might draw are endless. But beware, they are quite addictive to make. Before you know it, you will have made a whole series of spinners to impress and maybe even trick your friends with. Who knew that crafting could be so magical?

WHAT YOU WILL NEED

- Pencil
- Recycled cardboard
- Scissors
- Hole punch
- Markers
- Ruler
- Yarn or string

LET'S GET CREATIVE!

You can draw anything that you like on your thaumatrope. Try drawing a fishbowl on one side and a goldfish on the other. Does your goldfish swim in the bowl or jump out? Or how about a surfer standing on a surfboard on one side, and a big wave on the other? And if you don't have any string or yarn, or if you are having trouble spinning your thaumatrope, you could try building a thaumatrope on a stick. To do this, simply tape your drawings to a bamboo skewer, hold the skewer between the palms of your hands and rub it vigorously to make the pictures spin.

HIDDEN LEARNING!

Thaumatrope is an ancient Greek word that means "turning wonder." The two images on a thaumatrope appear to merge due to the scientific principle of "the persistence of vision," which means the speed at which the thaumatrope spins tricks your eyes into combining the images into one visual impression.

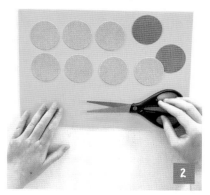
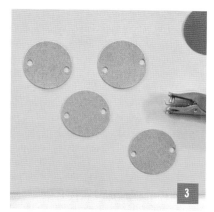
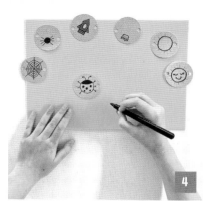
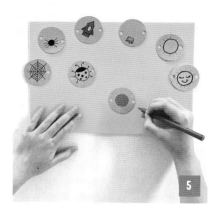

WHAT YOU WILL NEED TO DO

1. Search your home for a circular item that is approximately 2 inches (5 cm) in diameter. A recycled cardboard tube (such as a toilet paper roll) will work well for this. Trace the circle shape onto a piece of cardboard. You might like to make more than one thaumatrope, so trace a few circles onto the cardboard.

2. Carefully cut out each circle.

3. With a hole punch, carefully make two holes on each side of the circles. Make sure that the holes are at least ½ inch (1.25 cm) from the edge of the cardboard.

4. Think of a picture that you would like to draw. Draw half the picture on one side of the cardboard with markers. For example, if you want to draw a ladybug, draw the outline, black spots, antennae and legs for the ladybug on one side

5. Then turn the cardboard circle over and draw the other half of the picture on the second side. Using the example from the previous step, you would now draw a red circle for the body.

6. Measure and cut two 5-inch (12.5-cm) lengths of yarn. Tie the end of one yarn strand to one of the holes in the cardboard circle. Repeat for the other hole. To make your thaumatrope spin, quickly pull the yarn out to the sides so that it is taut while rubbing the yarn between your fingertips. This will make your cardboard flip and spin to create the illusion.

RELAX and CRAFT

Crafting can be so relaxing, wouldn't you agree? Spending just 30 minutes crafting, or even the entire afternoon, is the perfect opportunity to slow down and clear our minds. It can allow us time to process our thoughts and emotions. It also gives us time to recharge both physically and mentally. Crafting also develops creativity and is simply FUN!

Aside from the plain fun of it, crafting is an excellent form of mindfulness. Mindfulness is the practice of paying close attention to what you are doing in the present moment. It is being aware of your body, your thoughts and your feelings. Mindfulness practices can help you recognize and understand your emotions and keep them steady. These practices could even decrease anxiety and depression. Basically, mindfulness can create a feeling of peace and calm.

The crafts in this chapter will not only give you a chance to relax and practice mindfulness but will also result in amazing creations that you may like to gift to other people. I will show you how to make Ojo de Dios (page 126), a beautiful yarn weaving that originates from Mexico and will look gorgeous decorating your family's walls. We'll also make Guatemalan Worry Dolls (page 128) that you can pop under your pillow before bed to help guard against bad dreams. And we will make some bright and colorful gratitude piñatas that you can surprise your friends with on their birthdays (page 136).

Creative Tip: You may like to set up your own calming and peaceful craft space in your home for you to create in. This may be as simple as playing calming music while you craft or making sure that your craft space is clear and uncluttered. Perhaps the color of your workspace is one that makes you feel happy! While you are crafting, focus on your breathing and remain unrushed. This will also help create a calming environment. After all, crafting is not a race—there is no rush to finish your beautiful creations. Enjoy the process!

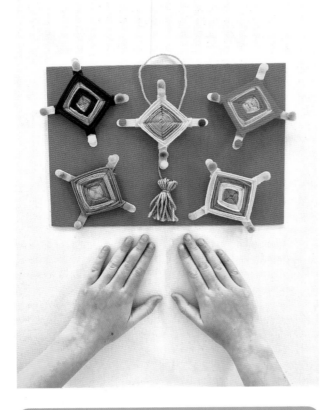

Ojo de Dios

The *Ojo de Dios*, or God's Eye, is an ancient symbol made by weaving a design out of yarn upon a wooden cross. They are commonly found in Mexican and Bolivian communities. Ojo de Dios are such fun to make, especially when you use several brightly colored yarns to weave together. Wrapping the yarn around the craft sticks is so relaxing and peaceful! The Ojo de Dios that you will make here are super bright and colorful, especially when you decorate them with fun pom-poms and tassels.

WHAT YOU WILL NEED

- White school glue
- Craft sticks
- Marker
- Measuring tape
- Scissors
- Yarn in several bright colors
- Pom-poms

LET'S GET CREATIVE!

You might also like to add a tassel to decorate your Ojo de Dios. To make a tassel, measure and cut a 10-inch (25.5-cm) piece of yarn and set it aside. Then take your ball of yarn and wrap the yarn around your fingers about 25 times. Snip the yarn from the ball and remove the wrapped yarn from your hand. Tie the piece of cut yarn around the top third of the tassel. Loop the yarn around a couple of times and tie a knot to secure. Snip the looped ends of the yarn opposite the knot to finish the tassel. Use the loose end of yarn to tie your tassel to the frame of your Ojo de Dios.

HIDDEN LEARNING!

Ojo de Dios were originally created by the Huichol communities of Western Mexico. They were made when a child was born, and then each year a new layer of yarn was added to the weaving. On the child's fifth birthday, the weavings were complete and hung in their home. The Ojo de Dios would watch over and protect the child.

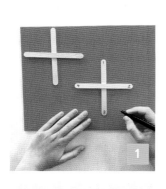

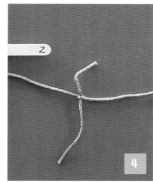
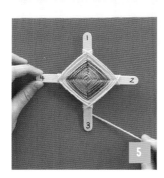
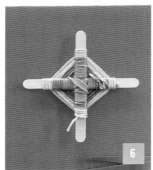
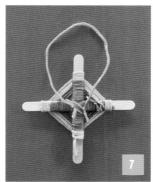

WHAT YOU WILL NEED TO DO

1. Start by making the cross-shaped base of the Ojo de Dios. To do this, add a drop of glue to the middle of one craft stick and press a second craft stick on top in the opposite direction. Allow the glue to dry. With a marker, label the sticks with the numbers 1 to 4 as shown. Don't worry, these numbers will be covered with pom-poms, so you won't see them on the finished piece.

2. Cut a 24-inch (61-cm) piece of yarn. Wrap the yarn around the center piece of the cross to hold the two craft sticks in place.

3. Keep wrapping the yarn, always moving in the same order around the craft sticks. First, wrap the yarn once around the craft stick labeled 1, then once around 2, once around 3 and then once around 4. Keep going around the cross to form approximately six rows of yarn.

4. Once you have wrapped six rows of yarn, snip away any excess yarn with scissors and tie the free end to a second 24-inch (61-cm) piece of colored yarn. You can cut these lengths of yarn as you need them.

5. Continue weaving the second color around the cross and then a third and even fourth—as many colors as you like. You can make each color the same length, or cut lengths with more or less yarn to add variety. Make the design your own unique creation!

6. When you have finished your weaving, secure the yarn to the cross with a knot and snip off any excess yarn.

7. Measure and cut an 8-inch (20-cm) length of yarn. Tie both ends to the back of the weaving to form a loop. You will use this loop to hang your weaving.

8. Glue some pom-poms to any exposed part of the craft sticks to decorate.

Guatemalan Worry Dolls

Guatemalan worry dolls are small handmade dolls that, according to legend, have the ability to remove worries from sleeping children. You simply tell one worry to each doll when you go to bed at night and then place the dolls under your pillow. In the morning, the dolls will have taken your worries away. These worry dolls are bright and colorful. Even if you decide not to put them under your pillow, they are certain to cheer you up!

WHAT YOU WILL NEED

- Pipe cleaners
- Ruler
- Yarn in several colors
- Scissors
- White school glue (if using googly eyes)

WHAT YOU WILL NEED TO DO

1. Start by making the body of the dolls with pipe cleaners. To do this, fold a pipe cleaner in half and twist it approximately 1 inch (2.5 cm) below the fold. Open the hole to make a circle. This will be the worry doll's head.

2. Next, take each free end of the pipe cleaner and bend them up to the top of the loop. Wrap each end around the existing twist and stretch the free ends out to form the arms. Squeeze the long loops together to form the legs.

LET'S GET CREATIVE!

You can attach your worry doll to some yarn to make a necklace. And if you do not want to make worry dolls, you might like to make a worry pet. To do this, rather than bending the pipe cleaner into the shape of a person, try bending it into the shape of a dog, cat or any other pet that you might like. And if you would prefer, you can actually wrap your pipe cleaners with strips of fabric to look like real clothes.

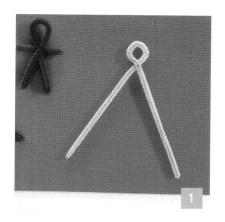
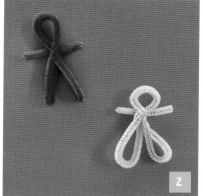

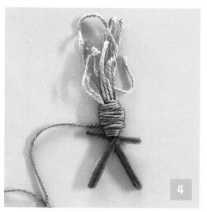

3. Measure and cut several pieces of yarn that are 5 inches (12.5 cm) long, and thread each one through the head loop. Tie with a knot to secure on the top. These pieces of yarn will form the hair of your worry doll. You can keep the hair long or trim it with scissors.

4. Starting at the top of the head loop, tie the yarn to the pipe cleaner and then wrap the yarn around the pipe cleaner, making sure that each loop is pressed up against the one before. Keep wrapping the yarn around until you have covered the face.

5. When you reach the body part of the doll, snip the yarn and secure it with a knot. Select a new color of yarn for the clothes. Tie your selected yarn to the pipe cleaner and start wrapping it around the body to make the shirt of the worry doll. Wrap the yarn around the arms and the body. Once you have finished the shirt, snip the yarn and secure it to the body with a knot.

6. Next, decide whether your doll is going to be wearing a skirt or pants. Select a new color of yarn and wrap it around the pipe cleaner legs to form the clothing. Now that you know how to make a worry doll, you can repeat the steps to make as many dolls as you like. Before you go to sleep tonight, tell a worry to one of the dolls, place it under your pillow and dream away!

Pet Cactus Rocks

Pet rocks are the easiest type of pet to look after! They don't eat very much, they don't make a mess, they're super quiet and they won't disturb your neighbors. Plus, they are fun to make! I arranged each of these ones into little planter pots of their own, so they look great sitting on a mantel or window ledge. And these cute cacti are not prickly at all—in fact, they are super sweet. As you are quietly painting away, you might even like to reflect on your mood and translate the emotion you're feeling into your little pet cactus's facial expression. For example, if you are feeling happy, paint big smiles on them!

WHAT YOU WILL NEED

- Smooth rocks*
- Green and white acrylic paint
- Paintbrushes (one with thick bristles and one with smaller, finer bristles)
- White school glue
- Googly eyes
- Small red or pink pom-poms
- Small planter pots
- Tissues or crumpled white paper

*Warning! It is safest to walk with an adult when you're outside on a nature hunt. Remember to cross roads safely and always pay attention to cars and bicycle traffic.

HIDDEN LEARNING!

Cacti grow in all shapes and sizes. Some are round and short, while others grow thin and tall. The very smallest cacti grow to less than ½ inch (1 cm) across. The tallest cacti can reach heights of over 66 ft (20 m). Cacti gather and hold water in their stems. The water is not pure, but is rather quite a thick liquid.

LET'S GET CREATIVE!

Try giving your cacti different emotions. How could you make them look sad, angry or excited? And of course you can paint any other type of flowers or plants onto your rocks, or even animals!

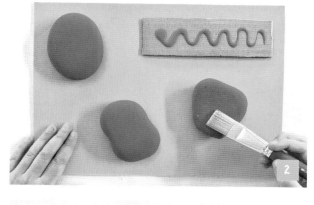

WHAT YOU WILL NEED TO DO

1. Head outside on a nature hunt and find the perfect rocks for this project. While any rocks will work, be on the lookout for smooth, flat rocks. These will be easiest to paint the face and prickle details on. And you will want them to be approximately 2- to 3-inch (5- to 7.5-cm) ovals. Once you are home again with your rocks, give them a quick wash in some warm soapy water to remove any dirt or debris. Let them dry before painting.

2. Paint your rocks green. Allow the paint to dry completely.

3. Next, take some white paint and paint cactus prickles onto your rocks with a fine paintbrush. The prickles can be simple dots or short brush strokes. Allow the paint to dry completely.

4. Glue on googly eyes and pom-pom flowers. Place the rocks in the little pots and display them so everyone can admire your adorable creation. If your rocks are too small for your pots, you can add some tissues or scrunched-up paper to the bottom of the pots to give them some height and allow them to be seen more easily. You may even like to decorate your pots with some brightly colored paints.

Yarn Hearts

These yarn art pieces are lots of fun to make and would be perfect for Valentine's Day or as a gift to someone that you love. You will only need to find some paper and yarn to make these beautiful hearts, and then just relax and quietly weave the yarn around the heart in all sorts of fun patterns. You could also paste miniature versions of these to a card as a gift or to a frame for displaying on a wall at home.

WHAT YOU WILL NEED

- Pencil
- 1 sheet cardstock
- Scissors
- Ruler and pencil (optional)
- Yarn
- Measuring tape
- Tape
- Beads

LET'S GET CREATIVE!

These yarn hearts would also look amazing sewn together into a garland! You could hang the garland in a special place in your house, or use it for a fun photo wall backdrop. And if you are feeling super creative, take a piece of recycled cardboard and make a giant string art piece. Imagine how impressive that would look!

WHAT YOU WILL NEED TO DO

1. Draw and cut out a heart shape from a sheet of cardstock. To make your heart perfectly symmetrical, you can fold your cardstock in half, draw a half heart along the fold and then cut it out along the non-fold side. Then when you open the fold, you will reveal a perfect heart.

   To make the instructions easier to follow, I have used a white piece of cardstock to make my example heart. You can use any color cardstock that you like.

2. Make small snips around the edge of the heart at ½-inch (1.25-cm) intervals. You do not need to be precise with these snips, but if you like, you can measure and mark these spaces with a ruler and pencil.

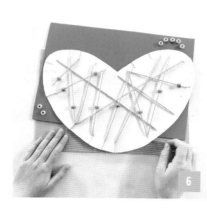

3. Measure and cut an approximately 24-inch (61-cm) length of yarn and place one end in between two snips. Secure the short end to the back of the cardstock with tape.

4. Wrap the yarn around the front of the cardstock and slip the yarn into a snip on the opposite side of the heart.

5. Continue wrapping the yarn around the heart. You can wrap the yarn randomly, or you can make a pattern. Be careful not to pull the yarn too tight or it may warp the card. Keep the yarn nice and loose as you wrap.

6. As you go, thread a bead every now and then onto the yarn and place it into a position that you like on the heart.

Slip the end of the yarn into a snip to finish and tuck the free end under the yarn. Tape the free end to the cardstock underneath the yarn to secure it in place.

Yarn Graffiti Monsters

These pieces of art are probably the easiest craft you will ever make and are just about mess free! They are a great way to use up all the pieces of yarn that you might have lying around your house too. I love the texture the yarn makes as you swirl it around the sticky contact paper. This really is a unique art piece that you will love putting together in a quiet, relaxing moment at home.

WHAT YOU WILL NEED

- Markers
- 1 sheet white paper
- Scissors
- Clear contact paper
- Washi tape
- Googly eyes
- Ruler
- Yarn

LET'S GET CREATIVE!

Of course, you do not have to make only monsters using this fun craft technique. You could very easily make a beautiful bunch of flowers or really test your creativity by making cool and colorful patterns so that your contact canvas looks like graffiti.

HIDDEN LEARNING!

The waves in the yarn give this art piece the feeling of movement and kind of remind me of a van Gogh painting. Have you heard of Vincent van Gogh? He was a famous Dutch artist who created the iconic paintings *The Starry Night*, *The Bedroom* and *Irises and Sunflowers*. You might like to create your own van Gogh–inspired yarn art.

WHAT YOU WILL NEED TO DO

1. With your markers, draw and color a monster onto a sheet of white paper. If you are having difficulty drawing a monster, ask an adult to search for cute monster drawings on the Internet for you, and choose your favorite as inspiration for your drawing.

2. Cut a piece of clear contact paper that is the same size as the white sheet of paper you drew your monster on. Place your drawing on a flat surface. Carefully remove the backing from the contact paper and place it sticky side up on top of the drawing. You should see your monster drawing underneath the sticky paper. Secure the sticky contact paper to your workspace with washi tape so that it doesn't move around as you work.

3. Place the googly eyes onto the sticky contact paper where the eyes are on your drawing. Be careful to place the eyes where you know you want them. If you need to move them, you can gently peel them off the contact paper and reposition them.

4. Measure and cut a piece of yarn that is 12 inches (30.5 cm) long. You will want to match the color of your yarn to the color of your drawing and only cut one length at a time.

5. Start by pressing the yarn around the outline of the monster, and then swirl the yarn to fill the monster drawing.

6. Once you have finished your monster, you might like to fill the background with some colorful yarn too. Remove the washi tape and then display your yarn graffiti monster!

Gratitude Mini-Piñatas

Surprise your friends with these cool and colorful mini-piñatas on their birthdays or special occasions. These are not just your average piñatas though! In addition to being filled with the usual sweets and confetti, they are also filled with little notes listing all the things that you love about your friends and their special characteristics. Your friends are going to love these super special and thoughtful gifts that you have made for them!

WHAT YOU WILL NEED

- Ruler
- Pencil
- Colored tissue paper
- Scissors
- Recycled cardboard toilet paper tube
- White school glue
- Tape
- Ribbon (curling ribbon works well!)
- 1 sheet white paper
- Confetti
- Wrapped sweets (optional)
- Pom-poms (optional)

HIDDEN LEARNING!

While piñatas are nowadays most commonly associated with Latin American countries, they may have actually originated from Asia. It is thought that Marco Polo discovered people in China building piñatas when he traveled there in the thirteenth century. They were decorated as animals such as cows, oxen and buffalo and covered in ribbons to welcome the New Year. Today, piñatas are used to celebrate all sorts of special occasions, including birthdays, Christmas and still the New Year.

LET'S GET CREATIVE!

These mini-piñatas would look amazing strung together on a garland or even sent home as a fun party favor! Try decorating your tubes with paint and markers so that they look like animals, or draw hearts for Valentine's or Mother's Day.

WHAT YOU WILL NEED TO DO

1. Using a ruler and pencil, measure and cut several pieces of tissue paper that are 4 x 7 inches (10 x 18 cm). Fold the strips of tissue paper in half lengthwise.

2. Fringe the ends of the tissue paper strips by making ½-inch (1.25-cm) snips along the folded edge of each folded strip.

3. Measure and cut two (2 x 2–inch [5 x 5–cm]) squares of tissue paper. Glue one square to the bottom end of the tube. Fold the excess paper around the tube and glue to secure. This will be the bottom of the tube that is pulled open by your friend or you when the piñata is finished. Set the second square of tissue paper aside.

4. Tape the fringed strips of tissue paper around the tube. Start at the bottom of the tube (the covered end) and work up toward the top of the tube.

5. Measure and cut a 10-inch (25.5-cm) length of ribbon and tape both ends to the inside top of the tube (the open end). This will form the handle of the piñata.

6. On a piece of paper, write your notes. Think about all the things you admire about the person you are gifting the piñata to. Cut out the notes and fold them so that they will fit into the tube.

7. Fill the piñata with your special folded notes, confetti, sweets and a few pom-poms (if using) through the open top end of the tube. Take the second square of tissue paper that you set aside in step 3 and glue it around the top of the tube.

8. Cut a 5-inch (12.5-cm) piece of ribbon and attach it with tape to the bottom of the tube. You might also like to glue a row of pom-poms around the top of the tube. To break the piñata, hold the tube by the handle with one hand and simply pull the ribbon on the bottom of the tube with your other hand. Watch the contents float to the floor!

Fabulous Family Flags

For hundreds of years, families have designed flags that represent their heritage. The designs are generally unique to each individual family in terms of the colors used and the symbols added. In this activity, you will get to interview your family and design your very own family flag that represents all the fun and crazy things that makes your family unique. Display your family flag at home with pride!

WHAT YOU WILL NEED

- Pencil
- White paper
- Ruler
- Colored felt
- Scissors
- White school glue
- Black marker
- 12-inch (30.5-cm) dowel to hang (optional)

HIDDEN LEARNING!

People sometimes refer to family flags as family crests or a family coat of arms. Family crests became very popular in the Middle Ages as announcers used them to introduce knights at competitions, and spectators could then distinguish each knight by these designs! The symbols on the coat of arms showed the knight's achievements. Traditionally, once a family chose a coat of arms design, it would be passed down from one generation to the next.

LET'S GET CREATIVE!

As an alternative, you may decide that there is one particular symbol that represents everyone in your family. You can cut this symbol out and use it rather than lots of little symbols representing each person.

WHAT YOU WILL NEED TO DO

1. Start by asking each family member their favorite color. Record this information on a piece of paper.

2. On a separate piece of paper, design your flag segments. You can divide your flag into any pattern that you like. You can do stripes, squares, rectangles, triangles or even a combination! Assign each segment on the flag to each family member's favorite color. My flag is the size of an A4 piece of paper, and I added four stripes to my family flag, one for each member of my family.

3. Using your plan as a guide, measure and cut corresponding pieces of felt. Glue the pieces together to make your flag.

4. Next, think about some of the symbols that best represent your family. Do you all like the outdoors, particular sports or special foods? Maybe someone in your house plays a musical instrument or loves to read books? Again, record this information on a piece of paper so that you will remember it for your flag design.

5. Draw your symbol designs for each family member onto a piece of felt with a black marker and carefully cut them out.

6. Glue the symbols onto the flag. Allow the glue to dry completely, then display your flag for all to see and enjoy!

Optional: If you wish, glue the dowel onto the back of the flag on one side. Older children might like to try stitching the felt symbols to their flag to make it look extra special and unique.

Shape Dream Catchers

These one-of-a-kind dream catchers will look so beautiful hanging on your bedroom wall. You can make any shape dream catcher that best suits your personality. Make sure that you hang these above your bed for protection against bad dreams so you can get the perfect night's sleep!

WHAT YOU WILL NEED

- White school glue
- Craft sticks
- Washi tape
- Scissors
- Yarn
- Measuring tape
- Beads
- Feathers
- Pom-poms (optional)

LET'S GET CREATIVE!

How would you make a traditional circle-shaped dream catcher? You could use an embroidery hoop if you have one at home, but if you don't, try twisting some pipe cleaners into a circle. For a nature-inspired design, head outside to find a thin, flexible stick that you can bend into a circle shape. Wrap the ends together with yarn or a piece of sturdy tape. With this type of dream catcher, you might like to tie on other natural items like leaves, flowers or even real feathers.

HIDDEN LEARNING!

Dream catchers were originally designed to "catch" evil spirits and tangle them up before they could enter a child's dreams. They are made with an open or "spider web" weave, in contrast to the Ojo de Dios weaving on page 126, so that the good dreams can easily pass through. Dream catchers were originally woven by Native American grandfathers and grandmothers and were placed above a sleeping baby.

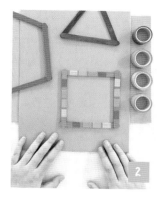
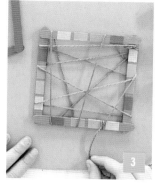
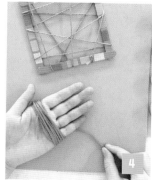
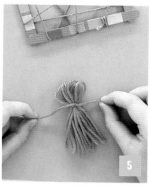

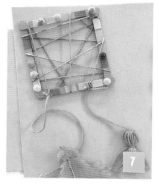
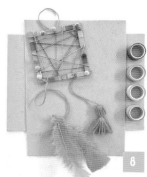

WHAT YOU WILL NEED TO DO

1. Glue the craft sticks together to make your shapes. Use three craft sticks for a triangle, four for a square and five for a pentagon.

2. Cut short lengths of washi tape and wrap the pieces around the craft stick frames for decoration.

3. Measure and cut an 18-inch (46-cm) piece of yarn and tie one end to a corner of the frame. At this point, you might like to thread a bead onto the free end and wrap the yarn onto the opposite side of the frame. Continue wrapping the yarn around the frame, adding beads and going in different directions. Make sure that the yarn is wrapped tightly. Tie the end of the yarn to the frame and snip the excess.

4. Think about how you would like to decorate your dream catcher. To make a tassel, measure and cut a 10-inch (25.5-cm) piece of yarn and set it aside. Then take your ball of yarn and wrap it around your fingers about 25 times.

5. Snip the yarn from the ball and remove the wrapped yarn from your hand. Tie the piece of cut yarn around the top third of the tassel. Loop the yarn around a couple of times and tie a knot to secure it. Snip the looped ends of the yarn opposite the knot to finish the tassel. Use the loose end of yarn to tie your tassel to the frame of your dream catcher.

6. Traditionally, dream catchers are decorated with feathers. To attach feathers, gather groups of two or three feathers and tie them together with yarn. Then thread two or three beads onto the yarn and tie the ends to the dream catcher frame.

7. You can also glue pom-poms to the dream catcher frame or add any other embellishments you have at home.

8. To finish your dream catcher, tie a loop of yarn to the frame so it can be hung on your wall.

Rainbow Hearts Wall Hanging

These pipe cleaner wall hangings take a little while to make, but wow are they worth the effort! The finished product is just amazing. This is an activity that you might like to put together over a couple of sittings, or share the workload with a sibling or friend to make a beautiful wall hanging together. Pipe cleaners are great fun to work with and are easily shaped into hearts. You will definitely want this art piece hanging on your walls at home! The repetitive nature of bending the pipe cleaners into heart shapes also provides a great opportunity to practice your mindfulness and calm breathing techniques.

WHAT YOU WILL NEED

- 8 x 11–inch (20 x 28–cm) piece black felt
- Ruler
- Scissors
- Pipe cleaners
- Hot glue gun* (or white school glue if you don't have a glue gun)
- 8-inch (20-cm) length of yarn or ribbon

Warning! Only an adult should use a hot glue gun. Have an adult help you with this, or use white school glue instead.

LET'S GET CREATIVE!

Now that you have the hang of bending pipe cleaners into heart shapes, you may like to challenge yourself and try sculpting all sorts of interesting shapes. You may like to form little rainbows or cloud shapes or anything bright and colorful to create a wall hanging that is totally unique!

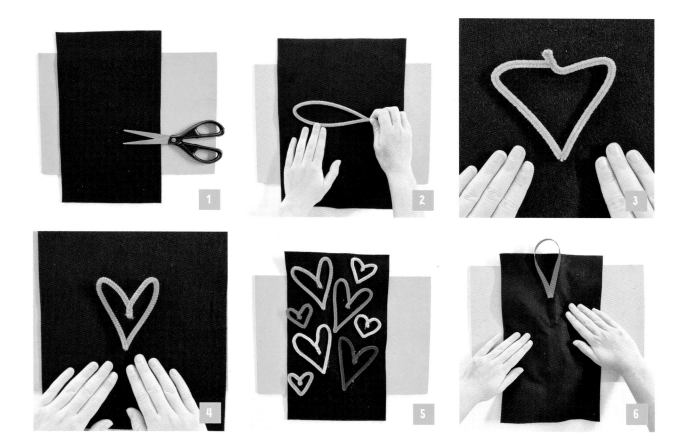

WHAT YOU WILL NEED TO DO

1. Place the piece of black felt on a flat surface.

2. Start shaping your pipe cleaners into heart shapes. To do this, bend a pipe cleaner in half and twist the free ends together.

3. Then press the twisted piece towards the bend in the pipe cleaner, molding the pipe cleaner into a heart shape with your fingers as you go.

4. To finish, fold the free ends of the twist over so that they are pointing to the inside of the heart. Repeat this step to fold as many hearts as you'd like. For my example, I could fit eleven hearts. Feel free to mix up the sizes of the hearts by cutting down your pipe cleaners to different lengths before you start folding them.

5. Arrange the hearts on the felt, placing them at different angles to each other and mixing up the colors. Once you are happy with their placement, ask an adult to glue them in place with hot glue, or you can use white school glue to glue them yourself. Allow the glue to dry.

6. Glue the ribbon or yarn to the back of the felt to use for hanging. Once the glue is dry, you can hang your masterpiece on a wall to display.

Upcycled Abstract Tapestry

Sewing is a really great skill for children to learn, and this simple, relaxing sewing activity is something anyone can make, even if you have never sewn before! You can use any fabric that you have at home, such as a piece of colorful fabric or even an old T-shirt. Just make sure that you check with an adult first before you start painting and sewing on your clothes.

WHAT YOU WILL NEED

- Scissors
- Cotton fabric or an old T-shirt
- Acrylic paint
- Paintbrush
- Ruler and pencil (optional)
- Yarn
- Tapestry needle*
- Buttons
- White school glue (optional)

Warning! For safety, it is best to have an adult help you use the sewing needle. Younger kids may need an adult to do the hand sewing for them.

LET'S GET CREATIVE!

Instead of painting simple shapes, you may want to try painting something a little more difficult. What about a lizard or a chameleon? Or even painting a whole scene with the animal in its natural environment? How amazing would that look?

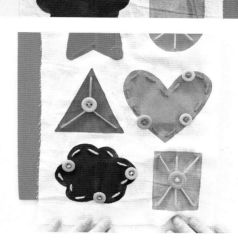

WHAT YOU WILL NEED TO DO

1. Cut a piece of fabric and place it on a flat surface. You can cut any size and shape fabric that you like. In my example, I cut a rectangular 8 x 12–inch (20 x 30.5–cm) piece of calico.

   Paint shapes onto the fabric and allow the paint to dry completely. I painted a circle, square, star, cloud, heart and a triangle onto my fabric. I actually painted the shapes on without a template, but if you want to be super neat, you could use a ruler and a pencil to draw the shapes on the fabric before you paint them.

2. Ask an adult to help you safely thread the needle with some yarn, then sew onto the colored areas of the tapestry. You can choose to sew around the edge of your colored shapes or add short random stiches inside the painted areas. I used yarn in the same color as the shapes I painted.

3. Next, ask an adult to help you sew some buttons onto the fabric. I color coded the buttons to the paint, but you can add your buttons to any area of the fabric that you like. If you don't feel confident sewing the buttons on, you can glue them instead.

4. Knot the yarn when finished and snip away any excess. This piece of art would look amazing in a picture frame, or you could cut a small length of yarn and glue it to the back of the fabric with the white school glue to form a hook to hang it from.

Templates

URSA MAJOR
Points north and is also known as
Big Bear and the Big Dipper

CASSIOPEIA
Is found to the south of
Andromeda

URSA MINOR
Also known as the Little Dipper
and contains the North Star

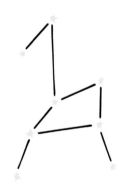

CAMELOPARDALIS
A faint constellation in the north
and is also known as The Giraffe

DRACO
The name is Latin for Dragon

ANDROMEDA
Sometimes called "The Chained Lady"

Acknowledgments

I am so very thankful to Page Street Publishing for allowing me the opportunity to put this book together. I am especially grateful to Sarah Monroe for her gentle encouragement, patient guidance and hard work molding my crafty ideas into this magical book. Thank you for trusting me to work with you!

BIG, BIG thanks to Steve, Josh, Isabel and Eliza, who live with piles of cardboard, glue and colored construction paper scattered around our house while I tinker away and create.

And finally, thank you to YOU, reader! I appreciate your support and hope that you have as much fun crafting as I do!

About the Author

Jacinta is an Australian mother, scientist and crafter. She graduated with a PhD from the University of Melbourne and worked in research, publishing articles in *Science* magazine and *Developmental Cell*. Today, she uses craft projects to communicate science to school students, as well as designing bright and colorful crafts kids can easily make just for fun at home! You can find Jacinta on Instagram (@cintaandco), on her blog (www.cintaandco.com) and on Facebook (Cinta & Co.).

Index